7 STEPS FOR DEFEATING BIAS IN THE WORKPLACE

Making Diversity Work

Revised and Updated Edition

SONDRA THIEDERMAN, PH.D.

KAPLAN PUBLISHING

New York

Vice President and Publisher: Maureen McMahon
Editorial Director: Jennifer Farthing
Acquisitions Editor: Shannon Berning
Development Editor: Joshua Martino
Production Editor: Dominique Polfliet
Production Designer: Todd Bowman
Cover Designer: Rod Hernandez

©2008 by Sondra Thiederman

Published by Kaplan Publishing, a division of Kaplan, Inc.
1 Liberty Plaza, 24th Floor
New York, NY 10006

Printed in the United States of America

May 2008
10 9 8 7 6 5 4 3 2 1

ISBN-13: 978-1-4277-9713-1

This book is dedicated to my grandchildren,
Aiden William Pierce McGinnis and *Eva Josephine Gray McGinnis*.

May you always remember to follow the sound of the bell.

CONTENTS

PART ONE
THE BASICS OF BIAS

PART TWO

THE VISION RENEWAL PROCESS

Introduction to Part Two   32

4. STEP ONE: BECOME MINDFUL OF YOUR BIASES   35

When a Filipino nurse sued the hospital, Carrie, his manager, had no idea what she had done wrong. Now, too late, she has become aware of her bias against Filipinos and admits she treated them poorly.

5. STEP TWO: PUT YOUR BIASES THROUGH TRIAGE   53

When Linda's bias caused her to lose a top sales professional to her main competition, she lost, along with a valuable employee, thousands of dollars in convention business.

9. STEP SIX: SHOVE YOUR BIASES ASIDE 111

Jill almost didn't hire Lance because he was over 50, and she figured he couldn't do the job. Luckily, she shoved her bias that, "older people are uncreative" aside and hired one of the most innovative professionals her department had ever seen.

10. STEP SEVEN: FAKE IT TILL YOU MAKE IT 115

No matter how hard Bess tried to stifle it, her bias that "people with accents are less intelligent" kept popping back up. Finally, she decided to treat everyone as if they knew what they were doing. The result? Improved performance and a bias that, this time around, went into permanent remission.

PART THREE

GATEWAY EVENTS™: ENTERING INTO DIVERSITY DIALOGUE

11. THE BENEFITS OF DIVERSITY DIALOGUE 127

Jane was hurt when she heard a rumor that her boss had made a sexist comment about her. She was tempted to say nothing and just quit. Instead, Jane stayed and told him how she felt. Now, they are both glad she did; it was all a misunderstanding.

12. GETTING DIVERSITY FIT 135

When the man in the wheelchair accused her of bias against him, the woman froze. What could she do? She knew he was wrong, but she was too diversity unfit to know how to respond.

13. COGNITIVE SKILLS FOR DIVERSITY DIALOGUE 141

When the presenter was finished, a woman walked up and accused him of bias because he had used the word guys *during his talk. What would you have done if you were the speaker?*

14. VERBAL SKILLS FOR DIVERSITY DIALOGUE   161

Certain she had lost the promotion because she was gay, Charmaine was ready to sue. She was certain, that is, until her boss showed his respect for her by really listening to what she had to say.

FOREWORD

by Michael I. Critelli, Executive Chairman, Pitney Bowes, Inc.

I have read many books and papers on diversity and have been part of many discussions on the subject as CEO of a company that has been at the leading edge of the subject. However, *Making Diversity Work: Seven Steps for Defeating Bias in the Workplace* truly advances the art of making diversity work.

Its title suggests that it is targeted to the workplace, but the insights offered go far beyond workplace diversity. Its starting point is that it is most important to understand others as complete individuals, not solely by reference to race, gender, national origin, ethnicity, sexual orientation, or disability. These attributes are essential to our understanding but should not limit how we look at others. Ultimately, every human being has a set of experiences and values that defines them, and if we are to be effective at interpersonal relations, we need to understand them better through conversation. By framing the problem the way she has, Dr. Thiederman makes it clear that every individual has the problem of biased attitudes, and that each of us can take steps to reduce bias.

Dr. Thiederman acknowledges that this task is uncomfortable, because it denies us the apparent safe haven of categorizing people permanently by one or more defining characteristics. She recognizes that we need some hooks on which to hang assessments of people from time to time, but she also points out the dangers of staying with static assessments. She points out that individuals are more complex and unique than any categorizations can indicate, and that they evolve over time as well.

Dr. Thiederman also challenges the notion that we are being nice to others by denying them in-depth assessments as unique individuals and by not sharing those assessments in candid but respectful feedback. She makes the commonsense, but often ignored, observation that we evidence more care and concern by telling others what they *need* to hear rather than by treating them as if they were fragile works of art.

We also can gain great insight from the frank way in which she points out that diversity works only if those who have been the subject of discrimination treat others with the same fairness and individuality as they should appropriately demand.

Dr. Thiederman is practical in giving the reader tools to move from a biased orientation to one that is as free from bias as human beings can achieve. Finally, she is helpful in recognizing that there are many opportunities in day-to-day interpersonal relationships for us to move from bias to a more individualized understanding of others, and that those "gateway" opportunities, as she characterizes them, while not easy to recognize or prepare for, need to be seized.

Her perspective is unique, very valuable, but very challenging. The best books I read take my thinking to a different level of knowledge and insight. This is one I highly recommend for those who want that kind of experience.

—Michael I. Critelli,
Executive Chairman, Pitney Bowes, Inc.

FOREWORD

by Richard M. Macedonia, Former President and CEO, Sodexho, Inc.

Diversity and inclusion are no longer new concepts in corporate life. They are incorporated into the culture of organizations because organizational growth and survival depend on them. In today's ever-changing global environment, organizations will either effectively leverage the increasing diversity or lose their competitive advantage.

I am pleased to say that because of its importance, diversity and inclusion are now a readily recognized part of human resource practices and policies and are increasingly aligned with business strategies impacting marketing and sales. A visible demonstration of the significant role that diversity and inclusion play in organizational success is evidenced by the presence of well-established corporate Offices of Diversity, led by experts, many of whom report directly to CEOs.

Consequently, and in keeping with other social influences, most of us as leaders of diverse organizations might now say that our collective diversity consciousness has been raised and that we actively engage in behaviors that foster a diverse and inclusive workplace. After all, we have our diversity training certificates, we sponsor and support employee affinity group activities, we mentor individuals, we recruit, employ, and manage multicultural team members, and we embrace a global workforce as the key to success in the multinational marketplace.

Having said that, I would suggest that in spite of this wonderful progress, blatant bias still exists. I would take it another step and say that these are not the most damaging influences, however. It is the subtle and subconscious biases that lurk beneath these behaviors that wreak the most damage, because they are more difficult to pinpoint, and more widespread.

This is the premise of *Making Diversity Work: Seven Steps for Defeating Bias in the Workplace*—and why this book is so timely and necessary. In it, Dr. Sondra Thiederman calls on us to ask self-directed questions to bring our deeply held beliefs to light. It calls attention to both positive "biases" and "guerilla" biases, both of which translate into "nice" behaviors, and therefore are dangerous and hard to spot. She also identifies shared values as a means of reducing bias, and offers practical tools and strategies for companies and individuals to reduce bias.

Behavior and practices are only part of what we need to do to truly address diversity and inclusion in organizations. There is a deeper level of awareness in which we need to engage to really understand the answer to this question: What do I really believe about diversity and inclusion? This is a complex question, but I believe that addressing it will allow organizations to get to the next level in their diversity and inclusion journey, where each of us is embracing diversity without even consciously thinking about it.

What we believe influences our attitudes and impacts our treatment of others in the workplace. It is when each of us honestly and courageously addresses our beliefs about a topic that is very personal, when we make ourselves vulnerable to learn from others who are different from us, and when we put ourselves in sometimes uncomfortable situations that we will go beyond the "right" behaviors to truly embed inclusion in the culture and fabric of our organizations.

Any corporate leader striving for a truly diverse and inclusive team should take to heart the ideas and tools presented here. I urge you to share them with your direct reports, your peers, even friends and family.

I wish you honesty, courage, and wisdom on your journey.

—Richard M. Macedonia,
Former President and CEO, Sodexho, Inc.

ACKNOWLEDGMENTS

From the length of these acknowledgments, it may look more like I am thanking the team that worked on the *Oxford English Dictionary* than a book of this length. I know brevity is the soul of wit and all that, but there is just no way I cannot thank the many people who helped bring both editions of *Making Diversity Work* to life. Whether it be emotional support, interviews, editorial help, research, or the supplying of the dozens of bits and pieces of information that make a book like this worthwhile, I could not have done it without the people listed here.

The majority of authors traditionally thank the most important people at the end of their acknowledgments—sort of like an Oscar acceptance speech in which the high school drama teacher comes first followed by parents, spouse, and, finally, a deity. I realize, however, that many people don't read acknowledgments through to the finish. Because of that, I decided to break with tradition and mention my most important person first: my husband, Tom Sandler. You will meet him and his diversity foibles from time to time throughout the book. He may, as you will discover, not be a perfect man when it comes to bias; but then again, who is? In most other ways Tom is amazing. It was Tom who encouraged me when I felt this book would never come to fruition and who, with both editions, took care of the bits and pieces of living while I plowed through the final weeks of the creative process. For that support, and a myriad of other things, I will always be grateful.

There would be no book, of course, if not for those folks who were generous and brave enough to share with me their embarrassments, successes, and even their bias disasters. That kind of openness is a lot to ask, especially in today's climate where "guilty till proven innocent" of bias is the order of the day. The initial batch of brave souls served as models for the composite characters found in these pages. I met them informally in the few moments following dozens of workshops and speeches on diversity that I have presented throughout the years. These contributions amounted to little more than snippets of thought and experience voiced casually at the front of the room or over cups of coffee and stale pastry. Despite their brevity, these tiny tales gradually seeped into my consciousness and formed a shape that eventually looked suspiciously like a book that had to be written.

Other contributors were more formally interviewed. In no particular order, these include the following people: Barbara Ceconi, Kurt Kuss, Steve Hanamura, Tony Polk, Elena Panduro, Krista Cabrera, Deborah Helm, Dr. Åke Sandler, Jane Sandler, Deborah Pourali, Gayle Brock, Amber Caffall, Prue Drummond, Josh McGinnis, Singer Buchanan, Susan Swan, Richard DeSiato, Martha Mason, Booker Izell, Kevin Moore, Duane Roth, Joan and Bob Pierce, Paco Sevilla, Shelley Schwarz, Cathy Rudd, Nancy and Bill Bamburger, Stephanie Britton, Jessica Moore, Jim Lonergan, Julie Madigan, Alexander Hicks, Cheryl DeLeon, Amy and Mark Jackson, Jim Adamson, Roger Ackerman, and Robert Marks Sr. In addition, I must extend very special thanks to Zhao Lin Chen, whose elegantly simple story of his new life in America reminded me why this country is so great and why we must continue our efforts to resolve the conflicts that have for so long divided us.

There are others whose existence refined my thinking and helped bring this narrative to life. Among these is my daughter, Shea McGinnis, whose way of looking at the world is just different enough from mine to keep me ever-growing and ever on my toes. Then there are those who taught me so much about myself including the mysterious Harvard graduate in Chapter 11 and Louis, who showed me that I am far from bias free. Other contributors to my insights are Manny Davis, the finest limousine driver on the eastern seaboard; the anonymous and possibly angry young man in that Westwood, California, gas station; my son-in-law, Gil Cabrera, whose Cuban heritage has taught me about the subtle differences in perspective that so readily enrich relationships; and finally, "Candace," who reminded me in some ways of my childhood friend Karen Johnson. By the way, in anticipation of writing this book, I tried and failed to locate Karen. Karen, if you see this, call me! I'll take you to dinner and, in honor of Candace, this time we'll do it right.

Because so much of the material of this book is rooted in current workplace events and individual experiences, previously published material played a secondary importance in my thinking. The one exception is Bruce Jacobs's marvelous book *Race Manners*—now, deservedly, in its second edition. *Race Manners* brings to the conversation about bias an uncommon blend of painful truth, practical solutions, and pure poetry. Thank you, Bruce, for writing a book that inspired me and informed my efforts in ways I could never have anticipated.

Any writer needs, however, not only inspiration but practical help. Fortunately for me, I had that in abundance. Wordsmith Robin Kilrain was invaluable to me in the editing of this edition. Thank you, Robin, for your precision and skill. Corliss Fong of Macy's, Linda Jimenez of Well Point, Punam Mathur of MGM Mirage, Rohini Anand of Sodexho, Henry Hernandez of American Express, Sandra Evers-Manly of Northrop Grumman, Ernest Hicks of Xerox, and researcher Michael Woodwick provided both support and valuable material. Then there are the family members, friends, and colleagues who helped in so many other ways, including by reading the manuscript with an eye toward making sure I hadn't gone off the deep end. These include Julie O'Mara, Claire Ginther, Alan Richter, Roosevelt Thomas, Price Cobbs, Anne Rippey, Åke Sandler, Joann Nowka, Shea McGinnis, Gloria Applegate, Barbara Deane, Michael Wheeler, Gretchen Van Mare, and Diana Rowland.

My thanks to agents Andrea Pedolsky and Laurie Harper for their guidance and professional expertise. At Kaplan Publishing, I was thrilled to work with Shannon Berning, who called on her considerable humor, warmth, and expertise to guide me through the often stressful and confusing process of putting together a second edition. Special appreciation goes to Joshua Martino, another member of the Kaplan team, whose expert and sensitive editorial advice clearly enhanced both the readability and value of the project.

Never to be forgotten is Joan Pierce, my friend and assistant, who has been my sidekick and unflagging support for over a decade. I am grateful to Joan for so many things, including holding down the fort when I complained of not enough uninterrupted time; tolerating my short-term memory failure over details, which I know made her job a great deal harder; and, of course, her insightful reading of the initial and subsequent manuscripts.

Although they are not here to see this publication, I also want to thank the pair of "ambivalent racists" referred to in Chapter 7—my mother and father. Although you will learn a lot about my parents in these pages, one thing that will not emerge is how they instilled in me the virtue of hard work. This was a lesson learned, not so much through discipline or elaborate reward, but through support and quiet encouragement. The support I remember best came from my mother, who, during those long study nights of my high school years, had a way of magically appearing from the kitchen bearing nourishment at the exact moment it was needed. That moment usually fell around two o'clock in the morning; the nourishment came in the form of a bowl of sliced bananas and cream, with just a little sugar sprinkled on top. Never once did she admonish me to go to bed nor say I needed my rest; all she did was bring the bananas and the cream—that was all the encouragement I needed.

And that brings me full circle to the people to whom this book is dedicated: my grandchildren, Aiden and Eva McGinnis. May there be an abundance of bananas and cream in your lives, and may you never ever lack for just a little (extra) sugar sprinkled on top.

TRUTH BE TOLD

When you read the phrase, "Hollywood High School in the 1960s," what comes to mind? If your head is filled with images of pink cashmere sweaters with matching skirts, 57 Chevys, and maybe a budding movie star or two, then you're on the right track. You're also spot-on if the faces you are picturing are mostly white. At this very moment, I am gazing at the pages of my Hollywood High School yearbook. In it, I can count exactly 13 students who are what we now call "visible minorities." That's only 13 out of a class of almost 500. Yes, going to high school in my part of town was very much a white experience.

One of those 13 nonwhite faces was a girl named Karen Johnson. Karen and I had been best friends in junior high. She was one of only two black kids in our neighborhood, and although I wouldn't admit it then, I must now confess one reason that I befriended her was that she was black and I was white. That made me just a little bit of a rebel, and I liked that. That was my first deception.

When the time came to move on to high school, Karen and I drifted apart. We pretended it was because of the natural ebb and flow of friendship at a formative age, but one of the real reasons we were no longer friends was because of her blackness and my whiteness. That was my second deception.

And on and on we go: deceptions, distortions, myths, and at the very least, naive statements that we offer each other about our feelings for people who are different from ourselves. Perhaps we pretend that we never notice the color of a person's skin; maybe organizations deny that bias can be hidden behind well-meaning efforts to accommodate employees of diverse backgrounds. Perhaps we honor false accusations of bias while ignoring the real discrimination that is harder to identify and tougher to resolve. No matter what form the distortion takes, these untruths are largely responsible for the lack of progress that corporations have made in removing bias from the workplace.

THE PROMISE OF PROFITABILITY: AVOIDING THE PRICE OF BIAS

Here's another untruth: A diverse workforce is good for business. Are you shocked that I would dispute that statement? Before you slam shut this book in disgust, let me clarify. That statement is wrong because it is missing two key words. This is more accurate:

A diverse workforce is not automatically *good for business.*

Although a diverse workforce is theoretically beneficial, it will never reach its business-generating potential if the workplace is riddled with bias. Biases, you see, inevitably tax our organizations in stifled creativity, lost revenue, and costly discrimination suits. Let's take a closer look at the potential benefits of a diverse workforce and at the toll that bias, if not properly confronted, inevitably takes on our organizations.

Diversity Benefit: Creativity and Innovation

First and foremost, a diverse workforce is potentially more creative and innovative than one in which all team members share the same background. As reported in the magazine *Scientific American Mind,* the divergent points of view that accompany any kind of difference result in a productive tension that, if managed effectively, can't help but give rise to more creative ideas. Not only do team members in these situations exert more mental effort, but the tension also forces them to look at additional aspects of the situation and, thereby, come up with more novel solutions.[1]

But what happens if the pervasiveness of bias renders members of the team too uncomfortable to speak up with their ideas? What if they fear those ideas will not be heard or respected? The result is no differing points of view, no creative tension, and no advantage to a diverse workforce. In other words, bias causes your organization to pay a huge price in the form of ideas that go unheard and unimplemented.

Diversity Benefit: A Positive Corporate Reputation

Studies show that both stakeholders and customers want to do business with organizations that care about diversity and manage it effectively. Managing diversity effectively means hiring employees of all backgrounds, using diverse vendors, and treating all people with respect. The University of Massachusetts Center for Social Development, for example, found that 87 percent of those surveyed would prefer to give their business to companies that hire people with disabilities. Harris Interactive came up with a similar response. The participants in the Harris survey were asked if this statement applied to them: "I choose to do business with companies that I know have a commitment to diversity." Of those who responded, 65 percent strongly agreed.

These results find further support in the experience of individual companies. Accounting firms PricewaterhouseCoopers, and Deloitte & Touche, for example, were told by several of their largest clients that the firms must maintain racial and gender diversity on their teams or the clients would take their business elsewhere. Law firms, too, are aware of the importance of maintaining diversity among their associates. The firms utilized by Shell Oil, for example, were surveyed by the company to be sure that each and every one of them had solid inclusion programs in place. According to Catherine Lamboley, Shell's general counsel, the company actually stopped doing business with a couple of firms that, their survey revealed, were just giving lip service to diversity. Most dramatically, another organization won a $157 million Request for Proposal from an obviously important customer largely because one-third of its documentation was devoted to the issue of minority vendors. They won the client, by the way, despite the fact that their bid was not the lowest. It doesn't get better than that.

It is not only clients, however, who care about your company's diversity reputation, but vendors as well. For example, when Prudential was named to *Working Mother* magazine's "Top 10 Companies for Working Mothers" list, one of their vendors gave the company a substantial discount. This example alone illustrates the high value placed on diversity to today's marketplace.

Those are the perks for doing it right. What happens when a corporate reputation involving diversity is less than stellar? One obvious consequence is diminished revenue. Witness, for example, the loss to CBS of four major sponsors following the Don Imus "nappy-headed hos" comment in 2007. Another consequence is stockholder unrest, as exemplified by the proposed revolt of Wal-Mart investors at the June 2007 stockholders' meeting. One reason for the stockholders' dissatisfaction was the class action gender discrimination suit being brought against the company. That suit, by the way, was focused on the same subtle kinds of bias that are addressed in this book. These examples show that if we allow bias to flourish, we will pay dearly in a damaged reputation and, ultimately, reduced profits.

Diversity Benefit: Product Design

Another benefit of maintaining a diverse workforce is the prospect of developing products targeted to particular markets. This is not to say that every woman you hire knows what women will buy, or that every person who is blind grasps the needs of customers with disabilities, or that every Asian is versed in the needs of the Asian-American marketplace. To make those kinds of inflexible generalities is bias unto itself. It does mean, however, that some members of a diverse team have a deep understanding of the needs of certain consumers. Without that expertise, you could waste millions stumbling around in the dark to find what works in a rapidly changing marketplace.

The success stories in this area are numerous and the list still growing. PepsiCo's Frito-Lay division, for example, has a diverse product development team that works closely with the company's Latino affinity group to design products for the growing Latino market (currently at $860 billion in annual spending power). This partnership has so far produced Chile *Limón* Flavored Potato Chips and a product called Gatorade *Xtremo,* both of which are aimed at Latino consumers. According to the CEO, these products accounted for about one percent of the company's eight percent growth in 2004.[2] That success is impossible to ignore.

It is also impossible to ignore how failure to diminish bias in your workplace leaves you vulnerable to losing valuable employees and, with them, their unique knowledge and profit-generating ideas.

The Highest Price of Bias

Discrimination suits are every manager's nightmare. Even the most modest settlement—combined with attorneys' fees, Employment Practices Liability insurance, court costs, and loss of reputation—will take the gloss off anyone's annual report.

You may feel fairly sure that your workplace is free of blatant bias and discrimination. But what about the more subtle, and even unconscious, biases that often go undetected and unrecognized? They go unrecognized, that is, until they result in legal action.

Much has been written about whether or not Title VII of the Civil Rights Act of 1964, which is designed to protect employees from workplace discrimination, applies to these subtler forms of bias. Since 1999, however, when the case of *Thomas v. Eastman Kodak* was considered by the First Circuit court, general thinking has been that discrimination suits can be brought even if the bias involved was unconscious and subtle. In other words, subjective actions and decisions that result from unconscious bias can still be illegal even though the defendant did not intend to discriminate.

Every organization has the responsibility to protect its assets, be they human resources, ideas, reputation, energy, time, or, in the end, profits. This mandate can never be met unless we take on the accompanying responsibility of achieving and nurturing a workplace that is bias free and, therefore, hospitable to team members of all backgrounds.

WHO WILL BENEFIT FROM THIS BOOK AND WHAT WILL THEY GAIN?

This book might have been titled, *The Nice Person's Guide to Bias Reduction*. It is not about blatant discrimination, interracial hatred, or violent homophobia. These ailments are relatively simple to deal with, mostly because they and their perpetrators are easy to spot. They bring with them no gray areas, no subtleties of motivation, and few decisions to be made about the cure: ask the offender to leave.

Making Diversity Work is concerned instead with the subtler forms of bias that may be held by otherwise nice people (that's you, and me, and most of the folks we know). Such bias is insidious in the way in which it harms our workplaces, communities, and ourselves. Most of these biases lurk just below our conscious awareness, hidden from view by a reluctance to admit their existence and an inability to bring them to consciousness. Still, just because we aren't aware of these biases doesn't let us off the hook. Maybe none of us would dream of telling an antigay joke or firing someone because of his religion. But, to paraphrase Samuel Johnson:

> The tribe is numerous of those who lull their own responsibility with the remembrance of biases more destructive than their own. We must judge our individual virtue, not against the measure of those who fail, but against the elevated standard of those who succeed.

We need to maintain Johnson's "elevated standard," regardless of the type of diversity that surrounds us and the particular strain of bias that plagues us. This book will help you achieve this goal whether your issues pertain to ethnicity, disabilities, generations, personal appearance, religion, personality, gender, race, age, sexual orientation, or any other type of human difference. In particular, *Making Diversity Work* will be helpful if you are in one of these positions:

- *An executive* who is responsible for maintaining a competitive advantage, increasing productivity and innovation, and staving off costly discrimination suits
- A *manager* who currently wastes valuable time mediating bias- and discrimination-induced conflicts
- A *diversity director* who requires a fresh and practical tool for creating workplace harmony, increasing productivity, and educating people about how to make diversity work
- A *human resources professional* who is charged with recruiting and retaining qualified diverse employees and whose responsibilities include coaching and conflict mediation
- A *supervisor* who is responsible for accurately interpreting the needs and motivation styles of a diverse work team
- A *sales associate* or *customer contact professional* who needs to increase revenue among prospects of diverse backgrounds

- *An international business professional* who interacts with colleagues and customers from a variety of cultures

If you are seeking legal prescriptions for what is and isn't acceptable in the workplace, *Making Diversity Work* is not for you. You won't learn what words can be safely uttered nor what behaviors are actionable. You will learn, however, something far more valuable.

In this book, you will learn to diminish in yourself and others the fundamental attitudes that generate inappropriate or discriminatory behaviors.

Although we may never be able to create a perfect world or a perfect workplace, the goal of this book is to reduce bias to the point where we no longer need to be thoroughly schooled in political correctness or even specific rules of the law. Because our attitude towards our differences will be informed and enlightened, we will act unselfconsciously in ways that are respectful, legal, and effective.

AN OVERVIEW AND WHAT'S NEW IN THIS EDITION

Making Diversity Work is divided into three parts, each of which contributes a different element to the process of bias reduction. Among the background material in Part One, you'll find two chapters new to this edition. Chapter 1 addresses the following question: Can we use our rational minds to subdue, and even defeat, bias? Intended to convince you that your efforts will pay off, the chapter focuses on research showing that conscious decisions and strategic thinking can impact even the most subconscious biases.

Chapter 2 amplifies a topic that has received considerable attention since *Making Diversity Work* was first published in 2003: that bias can exist in people of all backgrounds. If the promise of this book is to be fulfilled, each and every one of us, regardless of the groups to which we belong, must make an effort to reduce our biases. To do otherwise will send the message that only certain biases held by certain people are harmful. Nothing could be further from the truth. The final chapter in Part One serves to overcome the many misconceptions about what a bias is, what it is not, and how to tell the difference. It is here that we learn that bias is an attitude, not a behavior, and that biases about desirable characteristics can wreak as much havoc as the most negative slurs. Also, this chapter introduces a previously unnamed brand of bias, *Guerilla Bias*™. Guerilla Bias is characterized by the fact that it—like the guerilla warrior who lies concealed within beautiful vegetation—hides behind kindly thoughts and seemingly compassionate behaviors. It is this type of bias that received the most attention since the publication of the first edition. In particular, managers were pleased to finally be able to name, diagnose, and attack a prejudice that has long prevented many of us from honestly and productively providing feedback to people who are different from ourselves.

Although the material in Part One is an important foundation, the heart of the book lies in Part Two: "The Vision Renewal Process." I chose this phrase because of the essential consequence of bias: it interferes with our ability to see people accurately—hence the need to renew our vision. The Vision Renewal Process consists of seven steps. It begins with strategies for becoming aware of our biases and moves systematically through the skills necessary to eliminate them. In the case of those biases that prove impervious to our efforts, strategies are provided that will, at the very least, minimize their impact on our work and our lives.

Whereas Part One is about information, Part Two is about skills. Because the skills found in the first edition seemed to fill a need for so many readers, I have enriched this material by providing more detail and more guidance for application. As before, you will find scattered throughout the text "Reader Exploration Points," which are intended to involve the reader and give him practice in the skills described in each chapter. This device has been particularly helpful to those who have used the book for corporate book clubs or diversity training. You'll find new "Workplace Application" sidebars, which provide practical ways that the material can be immediately applied in the workplace.

Those of you who are familiar with the first edition will notice that the chapter on kinship groups has been expanded and enhanced to contain more practical skills and workplace examples. I was driven to make this adjustment because of the strong response the notion of kinship groups has received and the change of climate that response reflects; namely, a shift of emphasis from how people differ to what they share. Both research and workplace experience supports the wisdom of this shift in that the identification of shared interests, values, and goals has proven to be a key strategy in bias reduction. The concept of kinships groups discussed in Chapter 8 is one way to implement that strategy.

Part Three ("Gateway Events™: Entering into Diversity Dialogue") continues the attack on bias, but does so from a different flank. This section provides the tools to carry on productive dialogue in the face of those awkward encounters that can happen when we work with people who are different from ourselves. The skills provided in this section not only serve to convert these sometimes painful incidents from disasters into "gateways" for better relationships, but they also reduce bias by enhancing communication and increasing mutual understanding.

This edition concludes with two appendixes. Appendix A, "Reader's Guide," summarizes the key points of each chapter and poses questions to the reader. This section has proved invaluable to those seeking to use the book in leadership or diversity training, or as part of regular management meetings and employee orientations. The second appendix, "Training Activities," is new to this edition. Because of how widely the first book was used in training, it was decided to include activities designed to facilitate the discussion of bias in the training room.

"TERMS OF ART"

Without a shared language, however, all our efforts to rid ourselves of bias will be wasted. We need to clarify what lawyers call our shared "terms of art." Terms of art are words and phrases that communicate very specific ideas. The world of law requires this precision; so, too, does the world of diversity. Sadly, that precision is dangerously lacking. The adjective *sexist,* for example, has come to apply to people whose offenses range from commenting on a female colleague's appearance to banning women from the boardroom. *Homophobic* no longer applies only to those who denigrate same-sex partnerships; now it seems to include any heterosexual who feels a twinge of discomfort when around people whose sexual orientation is different from her own. That most damning of adjectives, *racist,* used to have impact when it referred to those who held the obscene belief that an entire population was inferior to another. Casual use these days has a person labeled a racist if she merely misidentifies someone's race or is ignorant of the latest group labels.

Because words like *racism, sexism, stereotype, homophobia,* and *prejudice* have become so vague and exaggerated, I have chosen to minimize their use and employ instead the term *bias* to encompass the essence of them all. For the sake of variety, I will from time to time use *prejudice, stereotype,* or *misbelief* as substitutes for *bias.* In Chapter 3, we will look at what does and does not lie within the parameters of these terms, but for now, this definition will get us started:

> *A bias is an inflexible positive or negative belief about a particular category of people.*

Another area of confusion within the lexicon of diversity has to do with the complex issue of what to call members of particular groups. Is it *Latino* or *Hispanic?* Is it *black* or *African-American?* Is *ladies* acceptable or does that imply a confinement to arcane roles and prudish social restrictions? Is a certain group called *white, Anglo, Caucasian,* or do we make a real project out of it and call them *Euro-Americans?*

Keeping terminology straight may be a chore, but it matters. Admittedly, our culture has carried all this too far—changing *manhole* to *personhole* and adjusting classic quotes from history to conform to the he/she doctrine is ridiculous—but, in most situations, respect for groups mandates the careful choice of terms. Terms are symbolic of proud origins, of position in society, and of who brokers power—and who does not. The problem is that not every member of a given group wants to be called the same thing. All we can do is make a reasonable and respectful effort to do the best we can. Hence my choices in this book of *black* not *African-American, Latino* as opposed to *Hispanic,* and *white* rather then *Anglo.*

One word I really dislike is that most archaic bit of jargon, *minority.* If there were ever a term whose time has passed, *minority* is it. Even the city council in San Diego, California, a relatively conservative community, voted to have the term banned from use in city documents, stricken from past documents, and exchanged for *people of color.* I am no fan of that phrase—it is limited in scope and awkward—but at least it doesn't carry the pejorative and antiquated tone of *minority.* To refer to a group as a minority is like calling the American West *wild,* Russia a *superpower,* or China a *third world country*. The term is particularly ridiculous in my home state of California, where no group is a majority. How can there be a minority when there is no longer a majority?

For these reasons, instead of *minority*, I have chosen to use *emerging groups*. This term was introduced in the first edition of *Making Diversity Work*. At that time, I had anticipated that the phrase would be widely received in the diversity community and even expected it to replace the antiquated *minority*. To be honest, that hasn't happened. I'm not sure why, but I do know that one person told me she felt that the term *emerging* still carried with it the connotation of being "one down." Another reason could simply be that some old habits are hard to break.

I am disappointed by this response because, in my view, *emerging groups* serves an important function by shifting the emphasis from past wrongs to current solutions and future equality. Also, it repositions the *oppressed* or *minority* populations in our culture from groups lacking in position to groups that are, more positively, moving forward to greater achievement and empowerment.

Another term I have coined is *kinship group*. A kinship group is any population that shares a self- or externally ascribed characteristic that sets it apart from others. This characteristic might be a shared occupation, hobby, sexual orientation, personal interest, physical ability, gender, race, ethnicity, thinking style, or any other unifying factor. Because it can apply to any characteristic, the term *kinship group* emphasizes and respects the complexities of what people share and how they differ.

One of the advantages of the phrase is that it allows each individual to be identified and valued in an unlimited number of human dimensions. It enables, for example, an Asian engineer who is also a mother responsible for her elderly parents to connect to other Asians. But it also allows her to connect to women of all ethnic backgrounds, to male engineers, and to anyone who is responsible for dependents of any age. *Kinship group* allows for group pride but does so without implying a state of victimhood; the phrase also encourages people to look for what they share. Another advantage is that it excludes no one; even white males form a kinship group and, as such, are included as much in the discussion of diversity as any other population.

Finally, you will notice that I use the word *target* instead of *victim* for those individuals or groups who have biases directed against them. This choice is dictated by the philosophical thrust of the book, which puts forth the belief that we each have a responsibility to resist being oppressed by the biases around us. As you will see in these pages, we are all targets of one kind of bias or another; but we become *victims* only when we allow that bias to defeat us.

THE CHALLENGE AND THE LEARNING

I come from a storytelling family. As far back as I can remember, we practically cataloged incidents that amused us, stroked our egos, contained a lesson, or simply made life more fun. I remember my father telling of a solar eclipse experienced on a winter day in the New Jersey countryside. He spoke eloquently of the ice crunching under his feet and the trees casting distorted shadows in the snow. I also recall my mother's recollections of her nursing days and the time she received a champion Airedale and a diamond watch from a grateful patient. Then there was the one about the Union Pacific Railway and my father's trek across the country to become part of the golden age of Hollywood in the 1940s. It is because of this penchant for storytelling that I decided to use stories and anecdotes to communicate the points in this book.

When my staff and I first set out to gather these stories, we anticipated an easy task. After all, people often come to me spontaneously to tell of their latest diversity encounter. Why would it be any different when we were actively soliciting their experiences? We couldn't have been more wrong. Gathering personal experiences became a real challenge. When asked, for example, "Can you share with me an incident in which you learned something about how to overcome a bias?" even those who were involved with diversity and worked with bias issues daily came up blank.

We heard, "Sorry, I can't think of anything," so often and from so many different types of people that we knew there had to be more to this blankness than just lack of experiences. After some consideration, we realized that despite their numerous encounters with bias, some potential contributors were simply unable to emotionally detach themselves enough from the events in order to analyze them and recount them accurately. This awareness made us realize still more how much this book is needed.

The interview process also led us to understand how afraid people are to confront the issue of bias, even—or especially—within themselves. Quite frankly, I don't blame them. To look honestly at a conflict, or even a relatively benign interaction involving bias, can be painful and frightening. Every such exploration carries the risk of learning something unpleasant about ourselves. I hope this book will provide the tools to make examining our biases less threatening and, therefore, more productive.

Once we adjusted our interview strategies—the questions we asked and the way we formatted them—to compensate for these barriers, the stories began to flood in. At that point, however, we encountered another problem: More often than not, what we received were tales of sexism, discrimination, and hurt feelings. Although I'm sure that the contributors were genuinely hurt by the incidents that they recounted, I doubt that the sheer number of victim stories provided an accurate perspective on the state of bias in the American workplace.

Less frequently recounted were incidents in which two people found an unexpected bond, solved an interpersonal problem with aplomb, or overcame a bias by working together. This proved to us the old adage that negative experiences compel us to talk in order to find relief; the positive just rests comfortably in our distant memory. Discouraging as these results were, they opened up an entirely new avenue of thinking about the dynamics of victimhood, the power of perception, and the importance of shifting the discussion from complaints about the problem to suggestions for solutions.

WHITE MISCHIEF

As I updated this introduction, I realized that it sure was ethnocentric of me to assume that everyone who read the first edition would understand the meaning of the term "White Mischief." This time around, let me explain. That intriguing phrase is actually the title of a book about British settlers who inhabited the aptly named "Happy Valley" region of Kenya during the 1920s. Apparently this rowdy crowd got up to all kinds of personal excess and other "mischief" during their stay.

I chose this phrase not because any mischief of my own comes close to that committed by the denizens of Happy Valley, but because it sets me up nicely to talk about how my own whiteness created its personal brand of mischief as I wrote this book. In short, try as I did, I had a heck of a time getting myself, and my whiteness, out of the way of the writing process.

Every story and every idea was filtered through my values and my perspective. I alone chose, combined, and edited the stories to be included. Although, every incident is based on what really happened in the workplace, I must admit that certain situations sparked my interest, others reinforced my point of view, and some were couched in language that appealed to my aesthetic sensibilities. In a few cases, I even played psychic and guessed what the characters were thinking—a practice I strongly discourage in real life. Each choice that I made was dictated by my own cultures and upbringing.

The most pertinent of those cultures is the way of thinking that comes with my white, middle-class background: I am a stereotype of whiteness. I was raised in the 1950s and 1960s in a largely white neighborhood; exactly two black (Karen Johnson was one of them), four Latino, and seven Asian faces smile from the pages of my high school yearbook. I grew up in a world in which the color "flesh" in crayons, Band-Aid bandages, or stockings meant an odd shade of sickly gray pink. I knew, by the way, not one nonhospitalized white person who was that color. And, of course, I knew no black or Latino or Asian person whose flesh tone even came close.

I've always acknowledged that my culture affected my decisions, but the process of writing this book really drove it home. This first became apparent while deciding what questions to ask my research subjects. It came into view again as I watched my reactions to the anecdotes that came my way. I remember one story in particular. I read it in Bruce Jacobs's book *Race Manners*. It is about a black woman who, because of the color of her skin, was followed around an expensive department store by the store detective. Outraged, she finally went to the customer service counter where she demanded that the manager cancel her charge account.[3]

My first reaction to that woman's predicament was to put it in the same category as the tale of another woman who was also regularly followed by store detectives. That woman was middle-class and white. She was fond of wearing smocks with big pockets and routinely carried a large satchel-like purse. Because of how she dressed, it was common and reasonable for the detective in her local department store to be suspicious and keep a close eye on her every time she, with her giant purse, walked through the door.

In truth, this woman was no more apt to steal than the irate shopper from *Race Manners,* but she did have one weakness: a perverse sense of humor. As soon as she noticed the detective following her, she would feign putting small items into her purse or pocket, and she found great pleasure in leading the poor man from department to department.

The woman with the silly sense of humor was my mother. For her, being followed by the store detective was a game; for the black woman, it was the height and depth of bias. The contrast between the two stories, and my reaction to them, helped me grasp how our own cultures distort our understanding of other people's experiences. I cannot be objective. But, then again, no one can. As you read, you will bring your own point of view and experience to the material. My reaction and how I treat an incident is from my perspective; you will read it from yours. The trick to minimizing that impact is the same as the trick for minimizing the impact of bias: know that those perspectives (and those biases) just might be distorting what you see.

ADVICE TO THE READER

Before you continue, I suggest that you do some preparation. Take a moment to think about what you're trying to accomplish. What prompted you to pick up this book in the first place? Perhaps your goal will change as you move through the volume, but by starting with a specific result in mind, even a changeable one, you will be better able to maintain your focus. Also, before you read each chapter, look at the "Reader's Guide" at the back of the book for suggestions about what issues to explore with each new topic.

A few words of warning: Reading this book is apt to make you feel the discomfort of self-discovery. You will wince when one person's story of prejudice reminds you of your own and destroys any hope you may have harbored of hiding from your biases. This discomfort may become so great that you'll be tempted to put down this book. When the going gets too rough, remember that these chapters are filled with stories about good people, good people who have admitted to having biases, faced up to them, and moved on to better relationships and better lives. You can be one of them.

As you read, keep an optimistic attitude. Any aspect of self-improvement, whether it be reducing bias or losing weight, requires some belief in the potential for success. This is not a supernatural or superstitious notion; it's a fact. If we feel we cannot succeed, we quite rightly, and economically, reduce the amount of effort we put into finding creative solutions. If we wallow in the past, indulge in guilt, and listen to naysayers who spout rhetoric about bias being a fatal and irrevocable flaw in human nature, we are doomed to defeat.

Also as you read, remain vigilant in your task. Mere desire to defeat bias is not enough. Desire is the driver; the rational mind is the tool. One without the other will get us nowhere. Together, they can't be beat.

PART ONE

THE BASICS
OF BIAS

1

BIAS BUSTING: IT CAN BE DONE

CHAPTER FOCUS QUESTION

Can biases be fixed or is our only choice to work around them?

"It's hopeless," my friend Jim said, "There's nothing we can do about bias except to wait for this generation to die off and a new one to come along." Even a man as erudite as broadcaster Edward R. Murrow believed we could never rid ourselves of biases; we could only learn to work around them.

Fortunately, both Murrow and Jim are wrong. Of course some people refuse to change. For each of those, however, there are millions who, given the right skills and enough determination, can correct their distorted visions and see the world and its people more clearly.

Those who argue that biases can't be fixed say that they are an intrinsic part of human nature and, therefore, impossible to eradicate. Every time I hear the phrases "human nature" or "We're only human," my hackles go up. To say that something is "only human" implies that to be human is to be incapable of change; it connotes that there's not a darn thing we can do to improve ourselves or our attitudes. I am more optimistic. I, and the researchers we will discuss shortly, believe that through aware-ness, knowledge, and plain old-fashioned effort we can, at the very least, reduce our biases to the point at which they have a minimal influence on our lives and work.

Sure, some biases are so deeply embedded in the mosaic of culture that it would take a jackhammer to dislodge them. But most of the biases that permeate our workplaces today are more tenuously held and, therefore, are ready targets for extinction.

In view of how much biases cost us and the fact that, as we'll see in the next chapter, they are found in all segments of the population, it's good news that we can do something about them. The research in this area is very rich, and an entire book could be devoted to the evidence that there is a lot we can do about bias. For our purposes, I have chosen three studies. The first focuses on the role that time plays in the extinction of bias. The second explores how what we force ourselves to think can actually have an impact on our biases. And the third takes the view that, despite our propensity to categorize, human beings can very quickly shift the categories we use.

A MOMENT MORE IN TIME

The man of the moment is William Cunningham, a psychologist at The Ohio State University.[1] Professor Cunningham's work, and the solutions it inspires, is rooted in previous research on how the brain generates biased responses to different groups. Addressing primarily race bias, but later broadened to other types of difference, these earlier studies found that when white people view pictures of black faces, the region of the brain that is responsible for wariness (the amygdala), responds with a sharp spike in activity. This spike amounts to a primitive "jumping to conclusions" about the nature of people different from ourselves. It is what has been termed an "instinctive bias." It is this physical reaction—the spike in response to groups different from ourselves—that gave rise to the belief that biases are part of our hardwiring and, in turn, the erroneous conclusion that they are unchangeable.

What Cunningham did was look at this early research and modify the methodology just slightly. He made a tiny change, but that change produced significantly different results, results that hint very loudly at the reality that there is indeed a great deal we can do to defeat our biases. As you read what Professor Cunningham found, keep in mind how his findings might be significant in today's rushed and stress-filled workplaces.

Cunningham's "tiny change" had to do with time. In the earlier studies, the faces were shown for only 30 milliseconds—removed so quickly that they could only be "seen" subconsciously. Cunningham decided to find out what would happen if the pictures were viewed for a longer period of time—525 milliseconds, still too brief for the conscious mind to grasp. And yet, the extended time was long enough to change the brain's response. Although there was still a spike when the different faces appeared, the spike was not in the alarm center, but in the part of the brain that controls rational thought.

The upshot of this—and the very good news—is that, if given long enough, the conscious and rational brain does have the power to override even our most primitive biased instincts. This explains why we tend to react with more bias when rushed and under stress in the workplace. There is simply no time to take a beat and settle down.

This conclusion sends a message that has immediate application in the workplace:

We must give the rational part of our brains a chance to get in gear before reacting instinctively to someone who is different from ourselves.

I'd like you to think about the role that time plays in bias reduction as you move through the book. We will, for example, talk about "watching our biased thoughts" in Chapter 6, an act that buys us some of that precious time. In Chapter 8, we'll discuss time in a different sense when we emphasize the importance of spending time together to form new bias-reducing kinship groups. Later, in Chapter 10, we explore how self-consciously behaving in ways that are inconsistent with a biased attitude can actually weaken even subconsciously held biases. The time required to decide to act differently is another delaying tactic that gives the rational part of the brain a chance to take over. Most important, though, is the fact that Cunningham's work shows us that just one extra beat taken before we act, just one extra deep breath, can mean the difference between a biased decision and the ability to see people, not as categories, but as individual human beings.

KNOWING WHAT QUESTIONS TO ASK

Professor Susan Fiske of Princeton University brings a similarly optimistic outlook to the power we have to overcome bias.[2] She, too, took a new approach to the old "wariness spike" experiments.

Fiske, and her colleague Mary Wheeler, started off with roughly the same methodology as her predecessors. She had white volunteers look at black faces in a yearbook while researchers measured the activity in their brains. The twist, however, was that Fiske gave the subjects specific instructions before they looked at the pictures. Each volunteer was asked not merely to look at the face and react to it, but also to speculate about several traits that the individual depicted might possess. For example, they were instructed to guess whether or not the person was fond of asparagus. A silly question? Of course, but that silly question—that involvement of the brain in looking at the person as an individual, not just as a member of a group—had an almost magical impact on the observer's response: there was no spike in the brain's alarm center.

Fiske concluded that the brain failed to send out a message of fear because of the nature of the instructions her team had given each of the volunteers and, in turn, the state of mind those instructions created. The volunteers perceived no threat because, in their minds, there was no group by which to be threatened. They were not faced by a monolithic and frightening black population, but by individual human beings with individual tastes (in vegetables, no less!).

Fiske's work has served up two large helpings of good news. First, she has proved that, despite the brain's hardwired impulse to categorize, we can use the brain against itself to derail that impulse. It is possible to change our thinking so that we see people as individuals, not just as members of a group. In short, our biases—our "inflexible beliefs"—weaken when faced with the task of evaluating someone individually.

The second piece of good news is that Fiske's strategy for manipulating the brain is straightforward: Get in the habit of asking yourself questions about, and, therefore, focusing on, individual characteristics, not group membership. This focus might be on interests, or tastes, or hobbies; the subject doesn't matter. What matters is that you are forcefully funneling your focus onto an individual and away from the group to which they belong.

Another way to trick the brain into thinking without bias is to interact with people in a way that forces you to focus on individual needs and wants. Let's use a bias against homeless people as an example: "All homeless people are substance abusers." Once that bias is in place, there is little to keep the believer from drawing that conclusion about every person they encounter slumped on the sidewalk, sleeping under blankets in an alcove, or begging for handouts.

What would happen, however, if that same biased person had the opportunity to work closely with a group of homeless people? She might, for example, volunteer to serve Thanksgiving dinner at a soup kitchen where, in order to do the job properly, she would have to focus on each individual. One diner might want mashed potatoes, another yams. One might hesitate to ask for more; it is the server's job to notice and overcome that hesitation. Another might seem rude and demanding; the server must assess if that rudeness is threatening or just evidence of a person who has difficulty communicating.

The goal of doing all she can to make Thanksgiving as pleasant as possible for every diner forces our server into seeing each person as an individual. That goal and the questions she must ask to achieve it deflect her ability to see this group of homeless people as all alike.

Fiske's research shows us that it is time for an agenda change. It is time, as we will see in Chapter 8, that we have more goal-oriented contact with people who are different from ourselves. During that contact, we need to encourage both ourselves and others to substitute questions that focus on individuality for questions about a group. We might, for example, begin to ask things like, "What does this individual like?"; "What does he need?"; "What will motivate this particular woman?" These questions, as you can see, are nothing more than broader versions of Dr. Fiske's seemingly silly query, "Does this person like asparagus?"

TEAM COLORS

Well, sports fans, this is where you come in. Psychologist Robert Kurzban, while working at the University of California, Santa Barbara, scored us some more good news about our ability to reduce biases.[3] First, Kurzban, like other scholars in the field, recognized that human beings are in fact compelled to categorize those who are different from ourselves. Working off this premise, Kurzban's project was designed to discover if individuals have the power to shift what those categories are or if we are doomed to view the world through a filter of preprogrammed and preconditioned biases.

In Kurzban's work, the emphasis was on skin color and race. But, as you look at his findings, remember that they apply to other types of bias as well. Here's how the study was conducted. It was divided into four parts. First, volunteers were asked to look at individual photos of basketball players on a computer. Although the players wore identical uniforms, the subjects were told that each athlete belonged to one of two teams and that the teams were recently embroiled in a brawl on the court. During the fight, each player said something insulting to another. That insulting statement appeared beside the player's photo on the screen.

In the second part of the study, the same volunteers were asked to look at the photos without the accompanying sentence and, from memory, match statements on a list to the appropriate players. In the course of making these matches, many mistakes were made. The interesting element in this outcome was that, when the subject paired the quote to the wrong player, it was usually to a person of the same skin color as the player who actually had made the statement.

Parts three and four consisted of a repetition of one and two, but with one key difference. This time, the players pictured were wearing either gray or yellow jerseys. When shown the quotes paired with photos and then later asked to recall the matches, there were still errors. This time, however, there was an important difference: wrong statements were attributed, not to a person of the same skin color as the actual speaker, but to someone wearing the same color jersey.

This result led Dr. Kurzban to conclude that the human mind is remarkably flexible. Even though all of the volunteers had spent a lifetime immersed in the notion of skin color as an important "category" of human being, it took just a few minutes of exposure to an optional classification for them to shift to another system. In short, Kurzban's work demonstrates that the biases we hold, the categories we are accustomed to using, can be changed.

This result—this proof of flexibility—is still more good news about bias. It means that our collective and individual efforts at bias reduction will not go unrewarded. For example, later in this book, I will discuss the bias-reduction value of shifting people in our minds from one kinship group to another and how that very act helps reduce bias. Like Kurzban's volunteers, who shifted their thinking from skin color, with its accompanying danger of full-blown racism, to the innocuous category of jersey color, we, too, through mixed affinity groups, shared goals, and creative interaction, can change how we classify the people around us.

TOO GOOD TO BE TRUE?

I know, I know, it is tempting to say something like, "This is too simple, too good to be true. Bias reduction has to be more complicated than that." Of course, in some cases, it is "more complicated than that." But, often, especially with the kind of biases that most of us hold, it is in fact that simple.

CHAPTER SUMMARY

- Early research into the alarm centers of the brain led us to believe that rational thinking has little power to defeat instinctive biased responses.
- Subsequent researchers have, however, used a variety of techniques to show that we do, indeed, have control over our biases.
- William Cunningham discovered that allowing research volunteers more time to react to pictures of visibly diverse people caused brain activity to move from the alarm center to the part of the brain where more reasoned decisions are made.
- Susan Fiske and her colleagues found that we can reduce our biases by consciously asking questions about the needs and characteristics of the individual human beings with whom we interact.
- Robert Kurzban was able to prove that, despite the conditioning of society and our inborn desire to categorize things and people, we are able, fairly easily, to shift individuals from one category to another.

CHAPTER

2

"BUT EVERYBODY DOES IT"

CHAPTER FOCUS QUESTION

Are biases only held by members of "majority" populations?

As you read this, you may be thinking that you are one of the good guys who sees past skin color and accent and lifestyle. You may have been driven to pick up this book because you are a target of bias, but certainly (or so you think) not because you are a perpetrator. Admittedly, you probably are more innocent than the man who commits a hate crime or the woman who uses a racial slur. I wager, however, that you have your own share of biases and, like the rest of us, have something to learn about seeing people more accurately.

No group is blameless when it comes to bias. Sure, some biases are launched from a more rarified height by the most powerful and hit their targets with greater force. But, ultimately, bias is bias. No one group's bigotry has any more or less importance than another's. Thus, these pages are devoted not one bit more to the task of helping men honor women than women honor men; to helping Christians respect Muslims than Muslims respect Christians; or helping whites respect blacks than blacks respect whites. This book is as concerned with reducing the biases of a person with a disability as reducing those of the fully abled; it is as directed at heterophobes as at homophobes. No one group is more a beneficiary or more a target than another.

In that connection, these pages are filled with all kinds of biases and all complexions of villains. White villains, Asian villains, gay villains, and even a disabled villain or two. Susan, an employee at the Equal Employment Opportunity Commission of all places, is one of these offenders. Here's what she says about some of her most disliked clients.

> I don't want to put one group down, but when I listen to EEOC complaints, it always seems that it is the black people who are most angry and unreasonable. It makes my job very difficult and sometimes I just stop caring.

White racist, you say? And such a misfortune that she is employed at that particular job? You may be surprised to learn that Susan is black, and she is also frustrated and overloaded. And, as is the case with so many of us who struggle against our own biases, she may not be such a villain after all.

If you still need convincing that the only bias we need to fight lurks in the hearts of the so-called Anglo-Saxon majority, consider what happened as I rode from the airport with the Jewish owner of a small limousine service. The driver was all too willing to dump his biased views on a total stranger.

> I had barely stowed my luggage when the man began complaining about his difficulties in getting reliable employees. He said proudly that he would hire anyone—blacks, Spanish, Greeks—anyone except, as he put it, "rag heads." Claiming that "they are all bums," he admitted, with little awareness of how this same scenario might have played out against his own immigrant parents, that "when they call and I hear the accent, I say the job is filled. As far as I'm concerned, those rag heads ought to go back to where they came from." When I asked him how he knew they were all so bad, this otherwise apparently intelligent man responded definitively: "I hired one once and he was no good. Once burned, I've learned my lesson."

I thought of this obviously frightened man on September 11, 2001. The events of that day no doubt fueled his hatred and his fear. It takes little imagination to picture the ugly scene should another of those whom he called "rag heads" ever again approach him for a job.

Another myth about bias pertains to men and women. Somewhere we got the idea that sexism only lurks in the intolerant hearts of the male of our species. Well, take a look inside this shuttle bus as it loaded up the first morning of a women-in-technology conference and you'll see how wrong this assumption is. Things were fine as long as there were only women on the bus. Then, suddenly, everything changed.

As the conference attendees gradually boarded the shuttle, every new female passenger was greeted with enthusiasm. Each was asked where she was from and what brought her to the conference, and was offered other verbal niceties designed to make her feel welcome. Also, more often than not, someone would move her laptop case and invite the newcomer to sit down. Then, as if he were an apparition from Mars, a man mounted the steps. He was about 40-years-old, white, five feet ten inches tall, pleasant looking, and, judging from his deliberate stare straight down the center aisle, more than a little uncomfortable. Why? Because not one woman greeted him. No cheerful hellos, no words of welcome, no polite inquiries were issued to relieve his discomfort, and most telling of all, not one woman offered him a seat beside her.

To be fair, that those women were so inhospitable does not automatically mean they were biased against men. As we'll see in Chapter 3, bias is an attitude, not a behavior. In the absence of mind-reading skills, there is no way I could know how they felt about this man or men in general. The only way to find that out would be to ask them why they were so cold to the lone male on the bus.

That is, in fact, exactly what I did, and what I found out was not good. During my conversations with several of those women, I heard biases like, "Men don't care about getting more women into technology"; "Men don't want to help women. What is he doing at the conference anyway?"; and,

"You know how men are. He probably was just here to spy." I learned something sad that day: sexism runs in both directions.

Susan, the limousine driver, and many of the women on that bus no doubt have had plenty of experience as targets of bigotry. You would think that they would have learned from that pain and been determined not to inflict it on others. Sadly, cases like these, and dozens of others throughout the book, show us that human thought processes are often not logical and, as one contributor put it, "Suffering does not always bring enlightenment."

CHAPTER SUMMARY

- One of the common misconceptions about biases is that they are held only by the so-called "majority" population. In fact, members of any group are capable of holding inflexible beliefs about particular categories of people.
- Although the biases held by the most powerful are apt to do the greatest harm, it is the responsibility of us all to work on the biases that we hold.
- It is a sad truism that being the target of bigotry does not immunize any of us from becoming biased ourselves.

3

BIAS DEFINED AND MISDEFINED

CHAPTER FOCUS QUESTION

What is a bias and why is there so much confusion about what the word really means?

A BIAS IS AN INFLEXIBLE POSITIVE OR NEGATIVE BELIEF ABOUT A PARTICULAR CATEGORY OF PEOPLE

Based on this definition and going solely by the information provided below, which of these people are guilty of bias? I don't mean might be biased or suspected of bias, but absolutely, positively guilty.

- *Case 1:* Juan, a 50-year-old manager, had occasion to interview a woman named Nancy who, at the time of their meeting, was in her mid-20s. After the interview, Juan said to his boss, "I'd like to hire her, but Nancy has quit four career-track jobs since college. We need someone willing to commit for the long run. It looks like some Generation Xers really do move around a lot."
- *Case 2:* It was the end of a long day at the diversity conference, and Eva was tired and ready to relax. Figuring that most of the people she knew would be in the hotel restaurant, she walked in

hoping to hook up with a dinner companion or two. Upon entering the room, Eva was glad to see that it was filled with conference attendees. There was one problem, however: Her friends were scattered between two large tables. At one table, everyone, like Eva, was white; at the other, everyone was black. Because she knew the folks at both tables equally well, she was faced with a dilemma. Where will she sit? If she were honest, she'd admit that her impulse was to go to the all-white table. It promised a little more familiarity, a little more comfort. In the end, she gave into that impulse and took a seat at the table with the folks who looked most like her.

- *Case 3:* Ayana, an immigrant from Ethiopia, had been working at the department store for only three months. One morning, she was approached by a tall, blonde woman who asked her to find a particular item in another size. Upon returning from her quest, Ayana walked up to the wrong customer and said that her size was unavailable. The woman looked at Ayana blankly; Ayana had mistaken one white woman for another.

- *Case 4:* When Harry heard his new neighbors speaking English with a Spanish accent, he guessed that they were from Mexico. After all, he figured, everyone else in his neighborhood had emigrated from Baja California. In a gesture of welcome, he packaged up some homemade chocolate chip cookies, knocked on the door, and made awkward conversation beginning with, "Hello, I'm your neighbor next door. Are you from Mexico? I vacationed there last year and it is a beautiful country." The couple became visibly upset at Harry's assumption. Obviously outraged, they defensively pointed out that they were from Argentina, not Mexico, and even went so far as to say something like, "How could you think such a thing?" Despite Harry's good intentions, his neighbors were deeply offended. It took months to mend the rift.

- *Case 5:* Being a lifelong lover of the blues, Mary was thrilled to be invited to a concert presented by her favorite artists. Upon arriving at the venue, she made her way to her seat, which was next to the only white person in the audience. At the end of each concert, the musicians had a tradition of inviting the crowd to shake something white in the air as a symbol of solidarity and optimism.

When the call came to perform this ritual, Mary realized she had forgotten to bring the traditional white handkerchief so, without missing a beat, she grabbed the man next to her and playfully started shaking him.

- *Case 6:* Cameron's colleagues were just a little hesitant to hire Ming for the newly created IT position. Ming had a solid university background, but the job required extensive computer skills and his formal training in that area was weak. When the committee met to make the final decision, Cameron spoke vigorously in Ming's defense saying, "Ming is very much a product of his culture, so I'm sure, like all Asians, he'll pick up the technology easily."

- *Case 7:* Miriam worked as a high-level administrative assistant and had had many bosses in her 25-year career; some had been men and some women. When asked which she preferred working for, she responded vigorously, "Oh, a man for sure. Women in powerful positions are just too demanding and controlling. Besides, once a female makes it, she forgets about helping the women who are still coming up through the ranks."

- *Case 8:* Len was in charge of hiring engineers for his division. Because of the large number of Asian residents in the community, his boss mandated that Len hire a certain number of Vietnamese and Chinese engineers within the year. As hard as he tried, Len failed to meet that goal. When asked why he didn't hire more Asians, he said that the ones whom he interviewed lacked the assertiveness necessary for the job. On closer examination, it turned out that Len had misread the applicants' lack of eye contact as a sign of passivity and indecisiveness.

- *Case 9:* Gerry was the manager at a business journal based in New York City. One of his writers was a young woman named Liz. Liz was a satisfactory journalist but not quite up to the standards of the organization. Because of this, Gerry had gotten into the habit of editing her pieces, rather than doing what he did with the men on his staff: sending their pieces back for rewrites. When one of those men asked Gerry why he hadn't edited their writing too, Gerry said, "Your situation is different. After all, Liz is a single mother, and you know they all have a rough time and deserve an extra break."

CASE 1: FLEXIBLE VERSUS INFLEXIBLE— JUAN IS INNOCENT

There are a couple of elements in this scenario that might have misled you into believing Juan was guilty of bias. For one thing, you might have thought him guilty because of his statement, "It looks like some Generation Xers really do move around a lot." If you look at this sentence closely, you can see that it is not a bias, but, instead, a "working generality."

Anthropologists prefer the fancier phrase, a "salient pattern of culture." A salient pattern is a trait that applies to a reasonable number of group members. To believe that "some women are biased against other women," "males tend to be more interested in sports than females are," or "many Generation Xers like independence" is not bias. They are working generalities and, as such, are not intended to apply to every single member of the group. In short, Juan's use of the word "some" gets him off the hook.

Another reason you might have thought Juan was guilty is that the characteristic he ascribed to Nancy (changing jobs often) could, if applied inflexibly to all Generation Xers, indeed be a reflection of a bias. This confusion highlights a key point that will help you in your efforts to accurately diagnose bias in others and yourself.

Bias is an attitude, not a behavior, and just because a word or action is consistent with a biased attitude does not automatically mean it actually reflects a biased attitude.

It is probably in the realm of the clumsy, ignorant, and insensitive use of words that this erroneous connection between an action and a biased attitude is most often made. "Some of my best friends are . . ." "You don't look Hispanic," and (said to a black man), "Gee, you're tall. You ought to play basketball," are all statements that most certainly have been uttered by people whose very souls are riddled with bias. These statements are, admittedly, "consistent with" a biased viewpoint. However, as in a court of law, "consistent with" is not the same as "identical to" or "proof of."

CASE 2: "JUST LIKE ME"—EVA IS INNOCENT

First, let me confess that I am the "Eva" in this example. Several years ago, I was the key player in an almost identical incident. Somehow that evening stayed in my mind all this time, probably because I felt just a little bit guilty about my decision to sit where I did.

As it turns out, I had no reason to be uncomfortable or feel guilty about what happened that long-ago evening. I know now that people being drawn to others like themselves is not necessarily a symptom of a biased attitude. If it were, the employees at one large hotel in Washington, D.C., would be in real trouble. Were you to look into a managers' meeting at the property, you would be met with a veritable United Nations of diversity: Latinos at one table, Vietnamese at another, Bosnians to the right, Iranians and Czechs and Poles scattered in clusters in the center of the room. Is it racism? It could be, but in this case it isn't.

Living in a nation in which segregation is a painful part of our history, we assume that the clustering of kinship groups is a sure sign that something is wrong. Do these groups feel uncomfortable with each other? Are they afraid or excluded or—our paranoia shouts—are they plotting something? It is time we bring a balance to this issue of being drawn to people like ourselves. We must learn when it is bias and when it is simple human comfort.

It is this desire for comfort and the wish to be with people with whom we identify that draws us to members of our own kinship group. A kinship group, as we learned in the introduction, is any population that shares a self- or externally ascribed characteristic that sets it apart from others. That characteristic makes us feel that we have things to share, that we can get along, and that we probably have something to say to each other.

Another reason for this desire to be with people like us is the same reason that people dread public speaking: *fear of death.*

I'll let those of you who are afraid of presenting in front of a group sit with that a minute: *death.*

You know exactly what I mean, and you probably feel a stirring of butterflies at the very thought of standing in front of an audience. Here's how this system, which feels like torture to some of you, works.

Public speaking involves exposing our intellect, our personality, and, come to think of it, our bodies to public evaluation. (Am I making you feel better?) Because of this vulnerability, performing badly in front of an audience results in what we experience as public humiliation. When this humiliation envelops us, our trembling subconscious spews up that most fundamental of fears: fear of exclusion from the group and the accompanying terror that, like a child abandoned in the woods, we will be deprived of the resources to survive. That is how deep the fear of public speaking can be and how primal the need is to belong to a kinship group.

Because it is so primal, it is fortunate that there is nothing intrinsically wrong with this desire for solidarity nor does it make us any more prone to being biased. In fact, those of us who have a strong sense of kinship identity tend to be the very people who are most receptive to the ideas and input of other groups. This may seem paradoxical, but scholars agree. Psychological researchers Joseph Ponterotto and Paul Pedersen, for example, say that having a healthy ethnic identity is essential to feeling good about other cultures. They write:

> Feeling confident in one's self, one's values and one's culture increases, rather than decreases, the likelihood of being interested in and receptive to the cultures of others.[1]

A healthy "ethnic identity," or what might be called "group self-esteem," is merely a more global version of that darling of pop psychology, personal self-esteem. Personal self-esteem, like group self-esteem, is central to our ability and willingness to be open to what, and who, is new and different. As psychological theorist Nathaniel Branden puts it, "Self-esteem expresses itself in an attitude of openness to and curiosity about new ideas, new experiences, and new possibilities."[2] It's really very simple.

If we have a firm sense of our identity and our worth, we are not threatened by new ideas, fresh values, and unfamiliar ways of doing things.

Because we do not feel threatened, we, in turn, have no need to resort to bias to protect us.

Reader Exploration Point: I can best illustrate this by putting you to work on a simple task: Think of someone you know well who you believe has solid self-esteem. I don't mean a person who is arrogant, but someone who is, quite simply, comfortable in his or her skin. Other than a strong sense of self, what characteristics does this person have? Take a moment to give it some thought.

You probably came up with adjectives such as *adventurous, interesting,* and *confident.* You most certainly recorded something like "receptive to new things and ideas" near the top of your list. This person is not obnoxious nor does he have a superiority complex. More likely, your chosen subject has such regard for, and faith in, his essential self that he realizes it is not necessary to appear or be perfect. He can genuinely consider alternative ways of doing things, listen to creative ideas from colleagues, and explore suggestions for changes in policy—all without defensiveness or hostility.

If we agree that personal identity and self-esteem allow us to be more receptive to alternative ways of thinking, it follows that Ponterotto and Pedersen are right: Group identity and group self-esteem make us more, not less, receptive to what other kinship groups have to offer. And that, in turn, means we are less apt to be biased against them.

Having said all that, a caution is in order here.

Being comfortable with your own group is not a sign of bias, but failure to make an effort to be with others is a mistake.

It is a mistake because, as we will see in Chapter 8, one of the key ways for you to stave off bias is to spend time with people who are different from yourself. In short, was I biased for sitting with other white people that night in San Francisco? No. Would I have been better served, in terms of building relationships and keeping bias at bay, if I had stretched myself a little? You bet.

CASE 3: "ALL WHITE PEOPLE LOOK ALIKE"— AYANA IS INNOCENT

Confusing one member of a group for another is often also erroneously thought to be symptomatic of bias. If we wanted to, we could jump all over Ayana, a woman who was not accustomed to being around white people, for mistaking one tall, blonde customer for another. In fairness, however, her error is nothing more than an example of the truism that groups of things or people that are unfamiliar look alike to our untutored eye.

Take wine, for example—cabernet, in particular. To me a cabernet is a cabernet is a cabernet. Each glass is like the next—a little pinker, a tiny bit sweeter—but any show I put on of knowing the difference is pure affectation. I have so little knowledge of wine in general, and cabernets in particular, that they all taste and look alike to me. To my son-in-law, however, a chef and wine enthusiast, the subtleties in taste, bouquet, and color are so varied that he would never mistake a California cabernet for one produced in France. The difference is that Josh is familiar with wines; his taste buds have met and made friends with so many individual cabernets that he can easily tell them apart. On the other hand, I could certainly give Josh a run for his money when it comes to noticing the differences between two antique desks or a pair of Labrador retrievers.

CASE 4: A REASONABLE ASSUMPTION— HARRY IS INNOCENT

Harry may be socially clumsy, but, if we judge only from what is written on the page, we have no reason to think him guilty of bias. In a perfect world, Harry would have asked his question about Mexico a bit more tentatively. He didn't, but that omission does not make him biased. Harry's only crime was drawing a reasonable conclusion (based on the country of origin of his other neighbors) and having it turn out to be wrong.

I'm not sure, by the way, that I'd give his new neighbors the same break. They clearly felt that being mistaken for Mexican was an insult. This reaction points more to their own bigotry against Mexicans than Harry's mistake does to any bias he might have against them.

Like Harry, Frank, the new doorman at David's New York City apartment building, drew a reasonable conclusion when he assumed David was a deliveryman for a local Chinese restaurant. Unfamiliar with the tenants and committed to maintaining tight security, Frank asked David for identification before letting him into the building. David, a Chinese-American who was carrying a large bag of Chinese food, was furious and accused Frank of racism.

It is understandable that David was upset—he had, after all, worked hard to afford his apartment. It is not, however, understandable that he accused Frank of bias. Frank's conclusion was reasonable in light of the fact that 95 percent of the apartments in his Upper West Side neighborhood were occupied by white people.

Frank made a mistake. One reason he made the error was that he had no time to consider his options. To avert a possible burglary, he had to act immediately; he had no opportunity to explore his heart and mind for the seeds of bias. Sometimes, like when walking down a dark alley, we simply have to play the odds that our assumption is correct. When Frank realized his error, he apologized profusely and let David go on his way. On the other hand, if, after seeing David's identification, Frank had continued to believe that David did not belong in the building or had he thought something like, "Asians should stay out of this part of town," it would be reasonable to say that Frank was a bigot.

The difference between an error based on the amount or type of available information and a bias is that the unbiased person who made the error is willing and able to change his mind in light of new evidence.

A word of caution:

It is unwise to act on every reasonable assumption that comes along.

If we did, we would be guilty of both legal and moral transgressions, such as promoting a man over a woman because of the possibility that the woman may quit to bear a child. There is, of course, no "reasonable" assumption more irrefutable than the fact that women are more likely to become pregnant than men. That does not, however, make it right (or legal) to act on the assumption that pregnancy will actually occur.

CASE 5: IN THE SPIRIT— MARY IS INNOCENT

A good sense of humor, comfort with oneself, and a willingness to laugh at the forces that divide our society have nothing to do with bias. When I heard this story from the white person who had been so warmly embraced, I fell a little bit in love with Mary. I imagine you did, too.

CASE 6: A POSITIVE BIAS—
CAMERON IS GUILTY

Surprised? Perhaps you let Cameron off the hook because he was saying a good thing about "all Asians." I understand that temptation. After all,
most of us would love to be able to, as Cameron put it, "pick up the technology easily." However, if you look back at the definition of bias—"an inflexible positive or negative belief about a particular category of people"—it
is clear that Cameron's attitude is as much a bias as if he had uttered that
time-honored classic, "All Asians are inscrutable."

An inflexible belief about a positive characteristic is equally a bias—
and equally as destructive—as those biases that assign a negative trait to
entire categories of people. Positive biases can, in fact, be more destructive because they, similar to the Guerilla Bias™ we will meet shortly, hide
behind a mask of kindness. If you are dying to see what kind of havoc they
can wreak, skip ahead to Chapter 5, where we will examine the price we
pay for even the "nicest" brands of bias.

CASE 7: BIAS FROM WITHIN—
MIRIAM IS GUILTY

The red herring in this case is that Miriam's inflexible belief was against
her own kinship group. Yes, even though she is a woman, she clearly har-
bors a bias that all women, once they have reached their goals, feel no
responsibility to help others climb the corporate ladder.

Intragroup bias is a brand of prejudice, like positive bias, that often
goes undetected. That's unfortunate because biases within groups not only
have the same negative impact as any other bias, but they also have the
power to seduce us into believing that bias is a viable way to think. If, for
example, enough people hear Jan refer to her Japanese relatives as "hot
off the boat," or Tony call other Italians "dagos," it is too easy to say to
ourselves, "Well, if they feel that way about their own group, I suppose it's
OK for me to as well."

CASE 8: IGNORANCE IS NOT BLISS— LEN IS INNOCENT

Len failed to fulfill his manager's request, not because of a bias against Asian engineers, but because of ignorance of a cultural variation in communication style. Nobody had ever explained to Len, nor had he made an effort to learn, that some Asians immigrants drop their eyes during interviews as a sign of respect. He assumed this lack of eye contact meant that the applicants were either lying about their qualifications or lacked the confidence to tackle the demanding duties of the job.

Len was ignorant. He was ignorant of a cultural difference, and that ignorance kept him from making appropriate hiring decisions. Admittedly, this lack of knowledge is an incomplete defense and needs to be remedied. Still, ignorance—dangerous as it can be—is a far cry from racism or bias.

CASE 9: GUERILLA BIAS™— GERRY IS GUILTY

Gerry would be very upset to learn of his guilt because he is one of the nicest of nice people. He has a good heart, never wants to hurt anyone's feelings, and likes to think well of others. The bad news for Gerry, and for those around him, is that he is a carrier of a particularly dangerous species of bias: Guerilla Bias.

One reason Guerilla Bias is so dangerous is that it is difficult to spot and, therefore, very tough to diagnose. Like the guerilla warrior who hides within stands of sweet-smelling foliage, Guerilla Bias lies concealed behind good intentions, kind words, and even thoughtful acts. In Gerry's case, his so-called thoughtful act was to edit Liz's manuscripts for her, rather than give her the opportunity to learn from her mistakes.

Another reason that Guerilla Bias, despite its soft persona, is so frightening is that it's based on the particularly destructive premise that certain groups are in some way, and for some reason, in need of special treatment. Because of this premise, it's easy to confuse Guerilla Bias with kindness—but there is a key difference. Guerilla Bias involves a belief that every single member of a particular group needs special treatment. A kindness, on the other hand, is directed at one person because of a given event or circumstance. Here are some contrasts between the two.

Example:

Guerilla Bias: "All people with disabilities are emotionally fragile, so we shouldn't ask about their physical challenges."

Kindness: "Joe has not adjusted to the injury that immobilized his legs and is not yet comfortable talking about the disability. We'll discuss it after a little more time has passed."

Example:

Guerilla Bias: "All single mothers are so overburdened by family obligations that we can't ask as much of them in the workplace."

Kindness: "Erika has just been widowed and left with three small children. She is having difficulty getting child care but is doing the best she can. She has asked me to lighten her usual responsibilities for a few months, and I have agreed."

Example:

Guerilla Bias: "All Latino immigrants come from a culture that does not value punctuality, so we can't expect them to be on time."

Kindness: "Alba is still adjusting to how we do business in the United States. Also, she is having a lot of problems with transportation. She's been late twice. Normally, I'd issue a final warning, but I'm going to give her one more chance. She's a good worker and is just having a little trouble adapting to the culture."

In Gerry's case, his attitude toward Liz was, even according to his own words, not based on her individual needs. Instead, it was based on what he thought were the needs of an entire group of people (single mothers). His reluctance to hand Liz back her work and ask for a rewrite engendered a terrible price. It deprived her of the opportunity to learn the skills necessary to become a better writer. To me this is the height of discrimination—a type of discrimination seen far too often in today's diverse workplaces.

Another way to understand Guerilla Bias is to compare and contrast it to more traditional notions of prejudice. Prior to the identification and naming of Guerilla Bias, biases were usually divided into just two main categories. One category involves a conscious bias accompanied by behaviors that have blatantly discriminatory impact. When Abby refused to hire Lester because she considered him fat and, therefore, figured he must be lazy, she was guilty of a deliberate and observable bias against people who are overweight. When a person who is guilty of conscious bias is confronted, she is apt to see nothing wrong with her assumption and say something like, "That's just the way 'those people' are."

The second type of bias is unconscious bias. Unconscious bias has many aliases including *implicit bias, spontaneous bias, automatic bias, naive bias,* and even the picturesque moniker *stealth bias*. Even though the person bearing this attitude is unaware of it, the bias still has a negative consequence that can be observed by the target of the bias. An example of this is when Jack "forgot" to consider Carolyn for a promotion. Carolyn was highly qualified for the job; she was also, according to our culture's definition, overweight. As Jack later realized, he had dismissed her from consideration because of an unconsciously held bias that excessive weight is always a sign of laziness and self-indulgence. When a person who is guilty of naive bias is confronted, he is apt to come back with, "I didn't realize I was being biased. I apologize."

Guerilla Bias is similar to unconscious bias in that the person is initially unaware that he or she is biased; it differs in that observers and those who are the target of the bias are also generally oblivious to what is going on. This is because the bias is disguised as a kindness. If confronted with a charge of being biased, the Guerilla Biased person probably replies with a heartfelt and sincere, "I'm not biased. I was just trying to be nice."

There are two reasons that I have put so much emphasis on Guerilla Bias. First, as we will see in Chapter 5, Guerilla Bias causes a great deal of damage in today's workplaces. This is happening mostly because the bias is so difficult to spot. Second, Guerilla Bias is exactly the kind of prejudice that is most apt to afflict the nice people for whom this book is intended.

IFS, BUTS, AND MAYBES

Defining bias is difficult; it involves a demoralizing glut of yeses and noes, ifs, buts, and maybes, each of which seems designed to drive us mad. *Yes,* being drawn to someone like you is normal; *no,* this impulse should not be completely indulged. *Yes,* it is OK to make a reasonable assumption about a person, *but* you are biased *if* you don't change your mind in the face of conflicting evidence. *Yes,* it is all right to be kind to an individual, *but* it is a bias if you do it solely because of the group to which he belongs. *Yes,* some behaviors do not reflect a biased attitude, *but, maybe* those behaviors should be changed anyway.

The simplest way to cut through all this muddle is to think of a bias as the small voice inside each of us that, upon meeting a stranger, whispers, "I've known someone similar to you before, so I know what you are like." Biases cause us to react not to individuals but to a motley succession of stereotypes and caricatures. We no longer see the person as he is because the bias blocks our view. Bias is the gremlin that seduces even the kindest of us into patronizing the person in a wheelchair and "graciously" devaluing the contributions of our elders. It causes us to gently—but oh-so-certainly— make those who are different from us feel just a little bit less whole.

CHAPTER SUMMARY

- Behaviors and words are not biased; attitudes are biased. Actions or statements that are consistent with bias may be inappropriate, but they do not always reflect a biased attitude.
- The key characteristic of a biased attitude is that it is inflexible.
- Because of the deep-seated need for group membership as a means of survival, there is nothing wrong with, nor biased about, being drawn to members of our own group. It is, however, unwise to confine our contact to those whom we think of as most like ourselves.
- When we are unfamiliar with a particular group of people, individuals within that group tend to appear alike to our inexperienced eye. Therefore, to mistake one member for another does not, unto itself, mean that we are biased.
- It is not biased to make a reasonable assumption about someone based on available evidence. If, however, we later gain information that contradicts our assumption and we then fail to change our mind, we are probably guilty of bias.

- Biases that apply positive characteristics to all members of a group can be just as damaging as those that involve negative attributes.
- Bias against one's own group is not unusual and, like any other bias, cannot be tolerated in the workplace.
- Although the situation does need to be remedied through education, an error made because of lack of cultural knowledge does not necessarily reflect a bias.
- Guerilla Bias is based on the premise that members of certain groups are in some way, and for some reason, in need of special treatment. Guerilla Bias is hard to spot because it hides behind kindly words and seemingly thoughtful acts.

PART TWO

THE VISION
RENEWAL PROCESS

THE VISION RENEWAL PROCESS

If we look closely at our definition of bias ("an inflexible positive or negative belief about a particular category of people"), we can see that defeating bias amounts to breaking what is essentially a nasty habit of thought. That's what bias is. It is a conditioned way of thinking created by imagined necessity and perpetuated by repetition. To break the bias habit, we need to undertake a program of awareness, exploration, and practice.

This is what Part Two is all about. It details a program called the Visual Renewal Process, which will help you become aware of your biases and then guide you step-by-step through the stages of ridding yourself of their influences. Essentially, what these steps will accomplish is to freeze-dry each target bias by taking the emotional juice out of it, thus reducing it to an inert lump that can be grabbed and tossed out of your thinking and out of your life.

Although this sounds complicated, the process is actually relatively straightforward. The reason it works so well and is so easy to understand is that it embodies a natural progression from one step to the next. These steps are so logical that you may have already completed some of them without realizing it. You probably can recollect previously held biases that have slowly dissolved through the years—no major revelations, no dramatic conversion experience, just a gradual fading away and an accompanying clearing of vision. If you were able to go back and observe that slow dissolution, you would no doubt find that, unknown even to yourself, you passed through several of these Vision Renewal Process steps.

Partly because of its logic, the Vision Renewal Process allows those who are naturally further along to start at a later point. For example, Step One ("Become Mindful of Your Biases") describes how to become aware of your prejudices. Perhaps you already are aware and can move on to decide which biases you want to target for extinction (Steps Two and Three). Maybe you have already chosen which biases to attack. If so, you can plunge into the next step of dissecting your biases to reveal their foundations (Step Four: "Dissect Your Biases").

Some of you will find certain parts of the Vision Renewal Process easier than others. This is because one of the strengths of the strategy is that it employs not only the intellect but emotion and experience as well. Very few of us are able to work equally efficiently in all three arenas. It is tempting to suggest you skip those steps that don't come naturally, but that would be a mistake; it just might be those very steps that are, because of their difficulty, the ones you need the most.

This is where courage comes in. It would be naive to say that it doesn't take courage to examine the damage our biases have caused, to question the veracity of some of the people we have most admired, or to broaden our definition of the group to which we belong. It would, however, also be naive to say that we can build productive workforces and satisfying lives without getting our biases under control.

No matter what your learning style, the Vision Renewal Process will, at some point, feel a little threatening. When this happens, take comfort from knowing that success does not require a complete mutation of who you are, a change of personality, or a shift in fundamental values. It does require honesty and effort and a willingness to face your fears, have new experiences, and, ultimately, break a painfully destructive habit of thought.

4

STEP ONE: BECOME MINDFUL OF YOUR BIASES

CHAPTER FOCUS QUESTION

How can I become aware of my biases, to target them for extinction?

Fyodor Dostoyevsky, in *Notes from Underground,* describes our penchant for self-deception.

> Every man has reminiscences which he would not tell to everyone but only his friends. He has other matters in his mind which he would not reveal even to his friends, but only to himself and that in secret. But there are other things which a man is afraid to tell even to himself, and every decent man has a number of such things stored away in his mind.

One category of Dostoyevsky's sequestered things is our biases, our secret and often unconscious beliefs that shape how we feel about other groups of people. I agree with Dostoyevsky that fear is the primary cause of this secrecy. The fear that prevents us from admitting bias is that of having to acknowledge, even to ourselves, that we may not be quite as nice as we, and others, like to think we are. Until we overcome our dread of looking like bad people, or at least like less-good people, we will be unable and unwilling to acknowledge our biases, name them, and target them for extinction.

Carrie, a nurse supervisor at a large medical center, was one of those afraid. In her case, fear prevented her from admitting that she had a bias against Filipinos. The result was litigation.

> I still don't know that a discrimination suit was warranted, but I'll admit I did look at the Filipino nurses differently. I didn't realize it at the time, but since I knew their training was not like ours, I figured it was inferior. Every time they made the slightest error, I'd exaggerate it in my mind and get all over them. No wonder they felt I was treating them unfairly. I was. At the time, I just didn't want to admit I was capable of bias. It just seemed that would make me such a bad person.

Well, Carrie can rest easy. The good news is that being guilty of bias does not make her, or any of us, bad people. Bias is a way of coping with a complex, stressful, and ever-changing world. Yes, stereotypes are bad because they block our ability to see others accurately. But most of the people who hold biases are multifaceted human beings, complete with virtues , sins, and everything in between. What makes a biased person bad, or at least unwise, is refusing to identify the bias and accept responsibility for getting it under control.

POSITIVE ID

The lucky thing about biases is that even the ones that are initially unconscious aren't very good at staying hidden. All but the most deeply buried reveal their existence at one time or another. We may only be favored with a fleeting glimpse out of the corner of our eye, but, if we are vigilant, that glimpse just might be enough to get the healing process started.

If, however, we are to capture this glimpse, we must be willing to face the painful, embarrassing reality that we are all capable of bias. I had just such a reality check not too long ago. It would be convenient to pretend that this incident took place far in the past, long before I took up the work of bias reduction. But if I did, I'd be lying. In fact, the incident happened within the last couple of years. You'd think at that stage of the game I would have known better.

The target of my bias was a black man named Louis, who had recently begun dating a friend of mine. In an effort to make Louis more comfortable in our largely white social circle, I chatted with him at a couple of parties. No response. I tried bringing up subjects that might interest him. Still nothing. I kept making excuses for Louis, saying things like, "He must be uncomfortable," or, "Let's give him a chance," and, "We need to try harder." My daughter, never one to keep her opinions to herself (I am proud to say), finally asked, "Mom, would you try this hard if he were white?"

At first I resisted Shea's criticism, but eventually had to admit that I was expecting less of Louis than I would if he shared my culture and my race. As it turns out Louis lacked not only social graces but several other virtues as well—all of which I would have conceded weeks earlier if I hadn't been so busy holding him to a low standard because of the color of his skin. I had to face it: I was guilty of the very same Guerilla Bias of which I accuse others.

In this case, it was my daughter who helped me face my guilt. Most of the time, however, we are on our own, and that's what this chapter is all about: providing the tools to identify your own biases. You will be glad to hear that becoming aware of most biases is a straightforward process—no shrinks, no psychotherapists need apply. It is a matter, as these actions illustrate, of practicing the art of observation and evaluation.

- Observe Your Thoughts
- Examine Your Thoughts
- Explore Your Attitudes toward Human Difference
- Observe Your Behavior

STRATEGY I: OBSERVE YOUR THOUGHTS

Biases, as we know, are attitudes. As such they live inside our brains waiting to be noticed, first as thoughts and then as actions. Some, the most subconscious ones, are so rude that they whiz from attitude straight to action so fast that we barely feel the breeze, much less notice what is going on. Lucky for us, most biases are more courteous and make the journey to thought and then to action at a civilized pace—a pace that allows us to be aware of their presence.

It is our job to examine those thoughts to see what they tell us about our hidden beliefs. This means we need to watch what we think. "How can I watch my thoughts?" you may be asking. "I *am* my thoughts; there would be no 'me' without them. And if there is no 'me,' there is no one home to do the watching."

This is an understandable question considering the nature of our culture in which thought and intellect are highly prized. The truth is, however, that we are *not* what we think. There is a "you," an awareness, that lies behind your thoughts that is capable of observing and chronicling your musings as they rush by. Give it a try, right this minute. Watch the thoughts that are coming into your mind. Maybe they go something like this:

> What is this woman talking about? I thought this was a diversity book, and all of a sudden we're talking about mind control or something . . . better remember to make that vet appointment for Jazz . . . I wonder where she's going with this stuff . . . wish I hadn't been so rough on Wong at the meeting last week; I know he's trying his best . . . wonder if he really feels comfortable here . . . so glad Eva liked the doll I brought her from New York; I sure am lucky to have a granddaughter like her . . . hope I can get the raise so we can put her in the private school . . . wonder if this book will really teach me anything about diversity; I sure hope so . . .

And on and on they roll, seemingly into infinity: thoughts, ruminations, speculations, worries, fantasies, ideas, and reminiscences. Thought is alternatively fun and horrible, irritating and entertaining. It is also a wonderful tool for survival and creativity. Thought is not, however, who we are.

We've all watched our thoughts before. Have you ever, for example, been asked to say the first thing that comes to mind when you hear the word *cat, house,* or *airplane?* You probably responded with *dog, home,* and *fly.* When you notice, and then say, the word that pops up, you are watching your thoughts. That's all there is to it; we do it all the time. It's just that when it comes to something more substantial than a parlor game—like becoming mindful of an attitude—we lose sight of how simple and familiar the process is.

The activity below provides you a chance to watch and record thoughts that might be clues to your biases. The exercise consists of a list of kinship groups to which I want you to react. (**Stop!** Don't look at the list until you are ready to do the exercise.) As you read each category, jot down the first characteristic that comes to mind regarding that group. There are just three rules you'll need to follow:

- Take only five seconds to come up with your response. If you can't think of anything by then, move on to the next category.
- Your first thought can be about a positive or negative characteristic.
- Resist the urge to edit or second-guess your response.

Most important, don't be afraid of your answer; no one will see the list except you. Also, don't jump to conclusions about what your response means. It may or may not reflect a biased attitude. We won't know that until we examine it further. Again, take no more than five seconds to respond to each item:

1. A person in a wheelchair:
2. A person who smokes cigarettes:
3. A Muslim:
4. A fundamentalist Christian:
5. A single mother with three children:
6. A 50-year-old white male in an expensive business suit:
7. A 23-year-old white woman:
8. A blind person:
9. A native of New York City:
10. A Latino immigrant:
11. A single father with three children:
12. A woman who is five feet six inches tall and weighs 200 pounds:

Did words like *helpless* come to mind when you saw the phrase "a person in a wheelchair"? Did you happen to respond differently to the "single mother with three children" than to the "single father with three children"? Perhaps there were some categories for which you were unable to come up with an answer. If so, good for you! This is probably the only test you will ever take in which a blank answer is the right answer. The harder it was for you to quickly think of a characteristic of a group, the less likely it is that you hold a bias against its members.

The point of this exercise is not only to become aware of your specific responses, but also to introduce your mind to the habit of watching first thoughts. The goal is to make this "watching" eventually become automatic—and even, most of the time, fun.

The next step in the process is to take the practice of watching your thoughts out into the world. There, instead of a list, you will have a variety of real people to whom to react. ***Here's the task:*** For the next two weeks, notice and write down the first thought that comes to mind when you encounter someone from another kinship group (Examples: What is the first thing you think of when you see an Arab name on an application? What hunches rise from your belly when you learn that your colleague is gay? What conclusions do you draw when you see a skin color, notice the slant of an eye, or spy a Phi Beta Kappa key dangling on a chain?). By the end of that two weeks, you will find yourself well on the way to forming a habit that will be invaluable in your efforts to become aware of, and eliminate, bias.

If Professor Cunningham, the psychologist we met back in Chapter 1, were reading this, he'd certainly see the value in the idea of watching our thoughts. Essentially, what Cunningham is suggesting is that the more time we have to settle down after an initial reaction, the more rational and less biased we will be. Watching our thoughts buys us some of that needed time. It may be only an instant, but that thin slice of time spent noticing our thoughts, our reactions to another group, just might give us a fighting chance at, not merely becoming aware of our biases, but making a conscious choice to derail their power to dictate our behaviors.

STRATEGY II: EXAMINE YOUR THOUGHTS

Watching our thoughts is important, but it is merely the evidence-gathering stage of our investigation. The next step is to examine that evidence, to determine if each thought is indeed a whiff of smoke floating up from a buried bias or, instead, an innocent recollection of what our culture at large says about the group.

Switch Groups

One way to do this is for you to look at each initial reaction and ask yourself this question, "Would I feel the same way about the meaning of this incident if the actor were of a different kinship group?" Here are some examples of how these examinations might work:

- A female executive shouts and pounds the table when speaking of the underhanded tactics of a competitor. You turn to the person next to you and whisper, "She sure is getting hysterical."

  Ask yourself this question: "If the executive had been a man rather than a woman, would I still have thought he was hysterical or would I have assumed he was justifiably angry?" If your answer is no—you **would not** have thought he was hysterical—you just might have a bias that tricks you into believing that women are more apt than men to get upset when under pressure.

- A colleague with a heavy foreign accent presents a proposal for a new product at the monthly meeting. You know he is a good employee, but you don't like his ideas very much.

  Ask yourself this question: "If the presentation were delivered by a colleague who did not have a foreign accent, would I have liked his ideas better?" If your answer is yes—you **would** have liked his ideas better—you could have a bias that makes you believe that people with accents are less educated and, therefore, less creative.

- You are a supervisor in a small manufacturing plant. One of your line workers, a Latina, is chronically late to work. You decide not to say anything because, once she is there, she does a good job.

  Ask yourself this question: "If the worker were any ethnicity other than Latino, would I still let the tardiness go?" If your answer is no—you **would not** let the tardiness go—you might have a Guerilla Bias that says, "Latinos don't value punctuality as much as other groups so it is asking too much to expect her to adjust."

You will find a sidebar in this chapter that highlights how to use a "Bias Spotter" to help identify your biases. The questions we have just seen are good examples of the kinds of tools a bias spotter might use to help you meet that goal.

Measure the Emotional Intensity of Your Thoughts

The next step in determining if your first thought is evidence of a bias is to see how much emotion is attached to it. The less emotion, the less likely the thought is to be biased. Let's say, for example, that you have often heard the stereotype that "all New Yorkers are loud." You didn't believe it, and hadn't experienced it on any level; you just had heard the words. Because of hearing those words, the phrase "a native of New York City" reminds you of the quality of loudness. So you write down the word loud—no emotion, just a word. Is that a bias? Probably not.

On the other hand, let's say that when you see the phrase "a native of New York City," or run into someone who falls into that category, you feel just a little bit intimidated. This, because of the emotion of being intimidated that is bubbling up from your subconscious, is a different story. The fact there is emotion increases the chance that you really believe that the quality of loudness applies to all New Yorkers. That feeling of intimidation slides you a step or two down the continuum from innocent word association to bias.

Reader Exploration Point: Here's a chance for you to again become involved with this process. The task is to pick from the previous list five kinship groups that triggered significant first thoughts. Beside each category, record any measurable emotion that you experienced when thinking about that group.

After you have completed this task, do the same thing in your workplace and community. As you exercise your mindfulness and watch the first thoughts that come to mind when seeing people who are different from yourself, be alert to the emotion that will, or will not, accompany each response. Sometimes there will be none—good for you. Other times you might experience a vague feeling of discomfort, fear, or even anger. Again, good for you. I say "good for you" because recognizing that feeling means you have had the courage to explore an emotion that just might be invaluable in your journey to rid yourself of bias.

Identify Previous Experiences with the Group Involved

One of the most reliable ways to analyze if an initial response is indeed a bias is to look at the nature of your past experiences with the group in question. You are essentially asking yourself, "Have I had any encounters with members of this group that might have created an inflexible belief about their characteristics?" If, to stick with our example of New Yorkers, your first thought upon seeing the phrase "a native of New York City" was "loud" *and* you have indeed known loud New Yorkers in the past, your first thought is apt to be a bias. If, on the other hand, you have never had that experience, you are more likely to be just repeating, but not actually believing, what others have said.

Examine How You React When Your Assumption Proves Incorrect

Another trick to assessing if a first thought is a bias is to ask yourself what happens when, on a given occasion, a member of that group fails to conform to your expectation. If you simply shrug, adjust your thinking, and then go on about your business, you are probably off the hook. If, on the other hand, you use one of the following techniques to prove yourself right, the odds are good that your expectation is an inflexible bias rather than just a casual first reaction that amounts to nothing more dangerous than a flexible working generality. We will talk more about how these work in later chapters, but, for now, take a look at each of these devices to see if it seems familiar:

1. You rationalize what you see to fit your expectation ("She may not be loud like other New Yorkers, but that's because she is restraining herself.")

2. You declare that this one particular person is an exception to the rule. ("Our CEO may support diversity, but he's only the white man around who does.")

3. You do something to create the reality of what you expected. For example, if your bias says that Asians do not make good managers, you might fail to send a team member of Asian ancestry to the necessary training. The result? When the time comes for promotions, she, just like your bias told you, is unqualified.

STRATEGY III: EXPLORE YOUR ATTITUDES TOWARD HUMAN DIFFERENCE

Observing and analyzing your thoughts as you think of and encounter other kinship groups is a good start toward bias identification. There is still, however, one more piece of evidence that needs to be collected. Before we bring charges of bias against ourselves, we need to shore up our case by examining how we feel about the notion of difference itself.

Generally, those who have few biases tend to be fairly indifferent to whether or not a person is different from themselves.

People who possess the virtue of seeing others clearly neither ignore the difference when it is pertinent to the situation nor put excessive emphasis on it. Where do you fit in this range?

When We Hesitate to "Notice" Pertinent Differences

My friend Elise shared with me an incident that would be comical if it weren't such a good example of how *not* to handle differences. It happened when a United Parcel Service driver came to the reception desk at Elise's work with a package for a new employee named John. John, you'll need to know to understand the point of the story, was the one black employee in the department.

When the driver asked where he could find John, the receptionist pointed down the hall to a cluster of men standing by the copy machine. The driver, never having seen the new employee before, inquired, "Which one is John?" Elise then watched with amusement as her colleagues spent three minutes trying to describe John without mentioning he was black. Impatient, Elise, much to her colleagues' dismay, announced, "John's the black guy over by the window."

There was a time when Jim Adamson, formerly chief executive officer of the parent company of Denny's restaurants, would have also been dismayed at Elise's candor. Adamson, whose tenure at Denny's included the period when the company was climbing out of a morass of discrimination suits, was heard to say, "You know, we need to be color-blind; we can't see color." Ray Hood Phillips, at the time director of diversity, reprimanded him with a gentle, "Jim we do have differences; you need to recognize that." Adamson learned from Phillips's admonition and claims that one reason Denny's made so much progress in the area of diversity is that it stopped pretending that everyone in the United States was the same.[1]

Adamson is right. Not everyone in the United States is the same; there is, in fact, more diversity here than in any other nation on earth. And when a difference is pertinent to the situation, it is perfectly appropriate, and nonbiased, to notice it. In John's case, the color of his skin was a reality that needed to be acknowledged in order to get the job done (the package delivered). The fact that Elise's colleagues at the reception desk were reluctant to mention, or (allegedly) even notice, that John was black is very possibly evidence of their own biased attitude.

Reader Exploration Point: Have you ever pretended not to notice someone's difference, even when that difference was pertinent to the situation? If so, what group or groups were involved? Were any of these the same groups about which you identified a bias in the previous activities?

Just as Elise's colleagues' reluctance to mention John's race does not bode well for their attitudes toward black people, our hesitance to notice a difference when it is pertinent might be another clue to our own biases.

Denying a difference, when it is pertinent to the situation, suggests that we might feel there is something wrong with that difference.

To ignore someone's disability or skin color or accent or gender is to imply that our feelings about the difference are so negative and potentially so embarrassing that we had best pretend the difference does not exist. In other words, denial of the difference, even to ourselves, can be a way to cover up how we really feel about it. If, for example, we secretly believe that having an accent means the speaker is stupid, what more effective way to keep that bias from showing than to pretend we don't notice the accent at all? If we look down on black people, I can't think of a better strategy for concealing that bias than to create the impression that we are such good people that our saintly eyes don't even glimpse color distinctions, much less denigrate them.

In this connection, I am proud to say that I did not deny the differences embodied in the young man who was wheeled into a spot next to me at a recent diversity conference.

> There was no ignoring the facts that Randy could not use his arms, that his legs were shriveled, and that he would need some help. I'll admit that at first I was a little befuddled. What do I do? Do I do anything? For the fleetest of moments, it crossed my mind to pretend there was no problem, no difference. Fortunately, that moment passed, and I knew it was ridiculous to deny that the man had a disability and that he would require some assistance.
>
> Once I made that adjustment, I proceeded to matter-of-factly ask Randy if he wanted me to move over one seat to give him more room. He answered that that would be a good idea, so he could lay the handout on the seat beside him. Curious, I asked him why he wanted to do that. He answered, again very casually, that, with the handout on the chair, he could turn the pages with his feet.

Had I succumbed to the urge to ignore Randy's difference, not only would I have put him at further disadvantage, but I would also have created a distance and self-consciousness between us. His disability needed to be acknowledged and accommodated. And accommodation is not bias; it is friendship and compassion and human respect.

> *If a difference is pertinent to a situation, it is our obligation to take it into consideration.*

To do otherwise is to deny an important part of a person's heritage, who they are, and what they have to contribute to our lives.

When We Notice Differences Too Much

Having said all that, it is also evidence of bias when we make too much of a person's kinship group. I wonder, for example, to this day, what the fact that the woman was "Asian looking" had to do with Harold's story about the real estate agent who sold him his new condo. I'm also curious why the loud football players who disrupted my colleague's client dinner at a fancy restaurant had to be described as "black." If my colleague were trying to distinguish a particular football player so I would know who he was, that would have been different. In this situation, however, mentioning skin color was as pertinent to the story as the chef's special or the name of the waiter's girlfriend. Perhaps skin color and all it meant to him were just a little too much on my colleague's mind.

This *Reader Exploration Point* will help you discover if you are guilty of the same distorted thinking. Take a minute to give it some thought. Have you ever recounted an incident and mentioned the background of those involved even though that information had nothing to do with the story? Could the fact you mentioned the identity of the kinship group mean that the person's ethnicity, religion, or sexual orientation was too central to your thinking? Is the group you mentioned one of the ones toward whom you had a strong reaction earlier in this chapter? If so, you just might have a bias on your hands and in your mind.

STRATEGY IV: OBSERVE YOUR BEHAVIOR

I have gone to great lengths to emphasize that a bias is an attitude not a behavior, and that not every inappropriate action reflects a bias. In fact, it is only the most blatant of offensive behaviors that provide us with reliable proof of an underlying bias. Having said that, there are some actions that, if observed, alert us to the possibility that a bias just might be lurking beneath the surface. Here are some examples of some suspicious behaviors:

- In general, when walking into a meeting, whom do you sit next to or approach? Is it apt to be someone who looks like you? Are there particular groups you tend to avoid?
- Whom have you hired and promoted lately? Do they tend to be from one group more than another? Is this balance more than you would expect to see, considering the demographic mix of candidates? If this is the case, you might be on the lookout for either a positive bias in favor of one group, a leniency bias that favors your own, or a negative bias that keeps you from assessing a person's qualifications objectively.

Workplace Application:
Create "Bias Spotter" Partnerships

Forming Bias Spotter partnerships is an effective way to increase an awareness of—and, ultimately, reduce—bias in your workplace.

The Mission: The mission of Bias Spotter partnerships is to facilitate the identification of biases that interfere with effective functioning and decision making.

The Benefit: Research has shown that accountability to another person is a key component of bias reduction. Not only do the observations of each partner serve to identify bias, but the very fact that another person is "on duty" motivates each partner to stay more alert to her own biases and to any inappropriate behaviors that might arise from those biases.

The Guidelines and the Spirit: The Bias Spotter strategy is not intended as a means of setting up a mini–police state. Instead, it is similar to a good two-way mentor partnership in that it is based on trust and friendship. In order for this process to be effective, these guidelines must be followed:

1. As in any good partnership, both parties must commit to the betterment of the team.
2. Both partners must be willing and able to make all observations in the spirit of mutual support; this is not about being accusatory or intrusive.
3. As much as possible within the policies of the company, all observations are to be kept strictly between the partners.
4. Both partners need to remember that a bias is an attitude, not a behavior—no mind reading allowed.
5. Bias Spotter partners need to be extra vigilant when one of them is functioning in a new environment. This is because a bias may be activated in one setting but not another. Partner A, for example, may not feel or show any bias toward immigrants when in her own department. But, when visiting another location and feeling less comfortable, she may.

6. Bias Spotter partners also need to be vigilant when a partner is rushed or working under an unusual amount of stress. It is at times like these that we crave easy answers and quick solutions. Biases, because they are so readily accessible, are a tempting ally when time is at a premium.

The Task: Each person is responsible for observing the decisions, words, and behaviors of his partner. He must comment to his partner if he feels the behavior is inappropriate and/or if he feels there might be a bias involved. If a questionable behavior is observed, the partner might probe deeper by asking questions like:

1. "That comment seemed a little inappropriate to me. I wonder, have you had any bad experiences with members of that group that might still be with you?" (If the answer is yes, there might be a bias at work.)
2. "Would you have made the same decision if the people involved were from a different kinship group?" (If the decision were different, it is possible that it was influenced by a bias.)
3. "If the person involved knew why you made that decision, would he respect your reasoning or would he feel discriminated against?" (If he would feel discriminated against, a bias is very likely involved.)
4. "Would you like your children or other loved ones to know why you did that?" (If not, that action might be influenced by a bias of which the person is not proud.)
5. "I keep noticing that you don't coach members of different groups equally. Do you have any thoughts about what that might mean about your attitudes?" (If the answer is that some groups need gentler treatment or can't measure up anyway, there might be a bias at work.)
6. "How would you feel if you learned that a colleague had done the same thing? Would you suspect her of bias? (If the answer is yes, your Bias Spotter partner should become suspicious of his own attitudes, too.)

(continued)

7. "I've been noticing that you seem to hang around only with people that are most like you. Do you think that means anything about your attitudes toward, or degree of comfort with, different groups?" (If your Bias Spotter partner answers this question in a undefensive way, there is a good chance that no bias is involved.)

8. "The last three people you promoted were from the same kinship group. I wonder if you might be favoring that group over another. What do you think?" (If your Bias-Spotter partner does not have an objective reason for the promotions, a positive or Guerilla Bias might have influenced her decision.)

- When deciding whom to send to training, do you find yourself sending people from some kinship groups but not others?
- When picking people for plum assignments, is there any group you favor?
- Do you catch yourself being "nicer" to members of any one group than to members of another? I'm not talking about being kind to one individual because she needs or deserves it, but, rather, treating an entire group more gently than another. If so, this could be a sign of Guerilla Bias.

Evidence produced by observing behaviors such as these is not unto itself conclusive. If paired, however, with other pieces of evidence, it might close the case.

CONCLUSION: LOOKING TOWARD THE NEXT STEP

Becoming mindful of your biases is an important first step. Indeed, for some people that is all it takes to get their bias out of the way. Most of us, however, need more motivation, and that is what Chapter 5 is designed to supply. There we will look at the price we pay for harboring these inflexible beliefs. When we're done, we'll realize that any small comfort our biases supply is never worth the price.

CHAPTER SUMMARY

- Many of us are reluctant to admit our biases because we feel that to have a bias means we are no longer good people.
- Although biases are not desirable, they are not, unless they are extreme, automatically signs of bad character.
- One way to become aware of our biases is to observe the thought that comes to mind in response to a kinship group.
- Once we observe a thought, there are several ways to analyze it, to see if it in fact reflects a biased attitude. One way is to ask ourselves if we would have reacted differently if the person we observed were from a different kinship group. Other techniques include measuring the emotional intensity of our assumptions, examining previous experiences with the group in question, and looking at how we react when our expectation about an individual turns out to be wrong.
- Those of us who put either too much or too little emphasis on the ways in which a person is different are more apt to have a bias against that person's kinship group.
- Clues to biases can also be found by observing our behaviors.

STEP TWO: PUT YOUR BIASES THROUGH TRIAGE

CHAPTER FOCUS QUESTION

Which of my biases are causing the most damage?

When my daughter was a teenager, I learned one important lesson: Don't sweat the small stuff. So her room was a mess and her hair was green; she was a good kid and that's what mattered. The same principle applies to healing your biases. Some matter, some (almost) don't.

As we saw earlier, everybody has biases—big ones, small ones, destructive ones, and (almost) harmless ones. We need to aim our guns at the biases that do the most damage. In short, pick your fights. For example, lighten up about the fact that you tend to think that "all professors are absentminded" or that "all French people are good cooks." These generalities may not be entirely harmless (nor was my daughter's green hair), but you need to expend your energy where it will accomplish the greatest good.

At the end of the day, the only reason to attack a bias is because it is harmful.

We need to first go after those biases that either cause pain or interfere with our ability to function successfully.

Just as injured soldiers on the battlefield are put through a triage process to discover who requires treatment first, your biases need to be triaged to identify which ones most urgently need your attention. This is accomplished by examining the damage and pain each one is apt to cause.

To make this triage process easier, this chapter provides six of the most common ways that biases compromise success in the workplace:

1. Does Your Bias Compromise Your Ability to Hire the Best People?
2. Does Your Bias Interfere with Your Ability to Retain Quality Employees?
3. Does Your Bias Interfere with Corporate Productivity and Individual Success?
4. Does Your Bias Interfere with Your Ability to Sustain Harmonious Teams?
5. Does Your Bias Compromise the Success of Your Sales and Customer Service Efforts?
6. Does Your Bias Put Your Organization at Risk for Litigation?

As you read through each section, stop to decide if any of your own biases might, in the past, have compromised your success in any of these arenas. If so, what were the details of the situation, and what would you do differently now? Also, ask yourself if any of your biases might create similar problems in the future.

DOES YOUR BIAS COMPROMISE YOUR ABILITY TO HIRE THE BEST PEOPLE?

Linda would have had to answer this question with a regretful yes. The human resource director at a prestigious hotel in Beverly Hills, Linda allowed her bias to interfere with a key hiring decision. The mishap occurred during an interview for an important director of sales position. Had we been watching the conversation, we would have seen a look of complete befuddlement on Linda's face. Despite her extensive professional experience, she found herself in a quandary.

Sitting across the desk from Linda was an applicant who, by anyone's standards, was perfect for the job: outgoing, articulate, and very knowledgeable of the hospitality industry. She was also born and raised in Japan. Therein lay Linda's problem. Because of Mariko's heritage, Linda's evaluation of her was grossly distorted by another set of qualifications, or I should say *mis*qualifications, that popped into her head and blocked her view of what Mariko had to offer. All Linda could see as she looked at Mariko was a hodgepodge of stereotypes right out of a Hollywood movie: shy, retiring, and soft-spoken. Certainly, to Linda's biased eye, Mariko was not a good candidate for a high-stakes sales position.

Linda had a choice to make. The best option would have been for her to shove her bias, and these fictional characteristics, aside long enough to see Mariko for who she was and hire her. Unfortunately, that wise move was not Linda's choice. Instead, she rationalized away Mariko's assertiveness, in an effort to prove her bias correct. Linda decided to let her bias rule the day and rule her decision: Mariko did not get the job.

This human resources director is a classic example of a person who not only has a bias, but also refuses to let it go—even when confronted with external evidence that contradicts what she believes. She was desperate to prove herself right. It took a little doing (and, remember, all of this is happening at lightning speed), but Linda was able to rationalize her bias into an apparent reality. She did this by saying to herself that Mariko was just pretending to be assertive because she thought that would get her the job. "In 'real life,'" Linda said to herself, "she must be shy and retiring and soft-spoken."

Linda paid an expensive price for this exercise in stubbornness. Shortly after the ill-fated interview, Mariko was snapped up by a neighboring hotel that then proceeded, with Mariko's help, to abscond with much of Linda's lucrative convention business.

There are other ways that a bias can compromise our ability to hire the right person. Take, for example, what happens with respect to people with disabilities. Legalities aside, if we were really honest, many of us would admit that we tend to define applicants who have serious physical challenges by one thing only: their disability. If we were wiser, we would realize that no matter how severe the problem, a disability is only one aspect of who the person is, and it represents only one small dimension of what she has to offer the workplace.

The following are three examples of just such people. Their names are Barbara Ceconi, Kurt Kuss, and Steve Hanamura, and they are, among many other things, blind. I'll admit that when we first met, I did define these three multifaceted human beings as blind. And that's OK because, at the beginning, that's pretty much all I knew about them. As I got to know them better, however, their other facets began to emerge. Now I think of them as, yes, blind (no miracles have occurred), but also as people with many other dimensions as well.

> *Barbara is many things.* A college graduate, a guide dog owner, a woman, a blonde, a writer, an educator, a professional speaker, a blind person, a stepmother, an elected official, an advocate, a consultant, a daughter, an aunt, a bicyclist, a pianist, a former diabetic, a wife, and a white person.
>
> *Kurt is also multifaceted.* He is a chef, a guide dog owner, a husband, a father, a blind person, a trainer, a college graduate, an ex-husband, a diabetic, a jewelry maker, a man, a professional speaker, a potter, a skier, a parent, a white person, and a consultant.
>
> *Steve's list is filled with variety.* He is a consultant, a trainer, a Japanese-American, a man, a father, a blind person, a husband, a runner, a bicyclist, a sports fan, a writer, a singer, a professional speaker, an author, a sports fan (he asked me to mention that twice), a biography buff, a Christian, and a son.

As the labor market goes up and down, spikes and dips, and does all manner of things to keep companies and human resources folks on their toes, one thing remains the same: We need to hire the best person for the job, a task that is impossible if we allow our biases to get in the way. Whether devaluing a person with a disability or cloaking an applicant in imaginary qualifications—good or bad—biases are the enemy that skews our choices, blocks our view, and costs us the talent we so desperately need.

DOES YOUR BIAS INTERFERE WITH YOUR ABILITY TO RETAIN QUALITY EMPLOYEES?

When Hector walked to the front of the auditorium following my diversity workshop at a California bank, I wasn't much in the mood to talk. It had been a long day and I was anxious to get to my room, order my beloved room service, and see what movies were available on pay-per-view that night. Hector, however, looked anxious to speak his piece, so I reluctantly put down my laptop and gave him my full attention. Now I'm glad I did. Here is what he had to say.

I've worked for this bank ever since I graduated college. I figured I'd be here the rest of my career. That is until the company decided to open locations in the Latino community and transferred me from my old branch on the West side. I was very successful before, but just can't seem to make this new assignment work. I'm thinking of moving to another company where I'd have a better chance to get ahead.

Hector, by the way, was one of five Latino branch managers who approached me with this identical complaint. Each one was promising and bright, and each was ready to quit because of the prejudice his manager had toward him. The managers' bias—in this case, one of the positive variety—contended that "all Latinos are familiar with, and care about, Latino culture." You could regard this as a compliment, if not for the fact that it isn't true of all Latinos. Hector, for example, certainly would dispute this generality and say something like, "There's more to me than having Mexican grandparents. I barely understand, much less speak, Spanish, and, quite frankly, the culture just doesn't interest me much." Because of his manager's bias, Hector was put in a job that did not fit his skills. He, therefore, eventually left the company.

A bad job fit is not the only destructive thing that can happen as a result of a positive bias. When a person does not conform to the positive qualities that we anticipate, there is a tendency for us to dislike him for not measuring up to our expectations. Hector's manager, for example, felt there was something wrong with Hector for not having the characteristic (familiarity with Latino culture) that he expected.

Are you ever the target of this kind of bias? Perhaps as a woman you are expected to love children; as a straight man, to like sports; or as a gay man, to be artistic. Fail to conform to these generalities and you are looked at as just a little bit strange. A common positive bias toward women, for example, reads, "All women value relationships and have, therefore, a nurturing leadership style." Because of this bias, women whose leadership style is authoritarian tend, as reflected in a 2007 gender-bias study conducted by Catalyst, to be disliked and "their behavior frowned upon."[1] That "little bit strange" or "frowned upon" can be enough to make a workplace feel inhospitable and result in your best employees going elsewhere, where their real strengths will hopefully be appreciated.

It gets worse. Just like negative ones, positive biases interfere with the accurate evaluation of employees during the interview process. If we expect the person to have a certain positive characteristic, we tend to see that characteristic even if it does not exist. Let's say, however, that our bias isn't so dense that it completely blocks our view and, despite our expectations, we are able to see that a particular applicant is not quite what we—or our bias—expected him to be. This is when a secondary problem kicks in, a problem that was isolated by Eileen Hogan at the University of Virginia. According to her research, the disappointment of the interviewer's positive bias not being fulfilled can cause him to unfairly evaluate the employee less favorably the next time around. It is as if our subconscious is saying, "Well, if you're not going to 'appreciate' my positive (if biased) expectations for you this time by conforming to them, I'm going to make you really work hard for any break in the future."[2]

Another problem with biases that assume positive characteristics is that the positive trait is often linked in our minds to a corresponding negative quality. Here are some examples of that yin/yang thinking:

- Those who see all gay men as artistic are prone to also believing them to be emotionally volatile.
- Those who see all Americans as ambitious are apt to also see them as greedy and materialistic.
- Those who think Asians are good at sustaining intragroup harmony also tend to see them as too passive to be good leaders.

I can think of few groups we glorify more than we do the Irish. But our infatuation is a double-edged sword. Yes, we declare with a winsome smile, they are charming, but they are also childlike. Yes, they are poetic, but they are also moody and temperamental. Everyone, of course, "knows" how creative the Irish are; how sad, we say, that this creative spirit leads them to drink. Does this, by chance, remind you of your own positive biases at work?

DOES YOUR BIAS INTERFERE WITH CORPORATE PRODUCTIVITY AND INDIVIDUAL SUCCESS?

Guerilla Bias and Self-Fulfilling Prophecies

One of the most frightening things about biases is that they can easily become self-fulfilling prophecies. If a manager believes that an employee, because of the group to which she belongs, has a certain characteristic or lacks a particular ability, darn if the manager doesn't subconsciously find a way to make that belief come true. The promising black fighter pilots who flunked out of flight school in disproportionate numbers would know what I mean. An investigation revealed that some white instructors felt that the black pilots lacked the skills to fly safely. As a result of this bias, and in a misguided effort to save themselves and the airplane, the instructors were grabbing the controls prematurely, thereby depriving the pilots of the chance to show their capability.[3] The result was "proof" that their bias was correct.

Most of us are in no position to grab anyone's controls, but we all have the power to actualize our biases through our failure to coach diverse groups appropriately. This is exactly what Susan's managers did. I met Susan, a Filipino nurse, when conducting a needs assessment for a New Jersey medical center. As Susan entered the tiny room that had been set aside for the meeting, she seemed anxious and ready at any point to flee the interview.

Susan looked at me with complete bewilderment as she struggled to explain why she and the other Filipinos on her floor were performing less well than the non-Filipino nurses. Practically in tears, she said, "Nobody ever tells us what we are doing wrong. I think they believe it will hurt our feelings or maybe they just assume we can't get it right. Sometimes it makes me feel like just giving up."

Roger Ackerman, former chairman and CEO of Corning, would have reacted strongly had he eavesdropped on this conversation. During our interview, he said to me, "The root of all evil is bad supervisors who give appraisals without being candid." I would modify his quote just a bit to say, "The root of all evil is biased supervisors who give appraisals without facing their biases." Because of the Guerilla Bias held by her managers, Susan, like millions of other potentially valuable employees, will never be able to move up in the organization and is clearly lost to an industry that is ever-hungry for qualified, dedicated health professionals.

Leakage and Self-Fulfilling Prophecies

Another way that biases can become self-fulfilling is through a process called *leakage.* This term is my verbiage of choice for a process in which small semiconscious or unconscious behaviors (sometimes called *micro-inequities*) leak from our biases and drip with often destructive force on those around us. Maude is a classic case of a manager whose bias leakage has practically flooded her department. Maude, you see, believes that "all Latino immigrants lack ambition and, although well-meaning, won't amount to much in the corporate world." Because of this bias, Maude ever-so-subtly treats these employees differently. For example:

- she doesn't say "good morning" to the Mexican immigrants on her team and maintains very little eye contact with them.
- she looks preoccupied or crosses her arms while they present their ideas.
- she fails to encourage them to sit in prominent spots during important meetings.
- she fails to respond after they present their ideas; she, instead, says a perfunctory "thank you" and moves on to the next subject.

- she gives them briefer and less detailed feedback than she does to other members of the team.
- she fails to ask them tough and stimulating questions about the projects with which they are involved.
- she fails to make the effort to pronounce their names correctly.

None of these actions, I'm sure you would agree, are blatantly egregious. If taken as a whole, however, they have the power—drop by drop by drop—to make the team member upon whom they fall feel devalued, diminished, and disempowered. This disempowerment eventually results in Maude's bias coming true. Her Latino immigrant employees do, indeed, lose their ambition and end up, just as she predicted, not amounting "to much in the corporate world."

Buying into a Bias: Internalization

Elsewhere in the book, I've made the point that biases cannot be allowed to permeate our workplaces, regardless of who holds them. I keep emphasizing this for several reasons including the fact that the more a bias is expressed, the more likely it is that the target of that bias will buy into it and come to believe it to be true. Once that happens another form of self-fulfilling prophecy kicks in: the person actually might subconsciously begin to adjust her personality and life choices to prove the bias correct.

This insidious process is called "bias internalization" and the following composite character is one of its victims. Does "Ms. She" sound familiar? Is she someone on your team? Is she you?

Everybody knew Ms. She was smart—in the top 10 percent of her high school graduating class. In addition, she combined competitive athletic ability and good social skills with an uncanny knack for winning every student body election she entered. She also had unusually strong career goals for her generation. That was in the late 1960s. Ms. She has long since lost sight of those career goals. Somehow, they just seemed to fade from view. She's not quite sure what happened, but she does know that her life did not turn out as she had hoped.

Our Ms. She is a combination of several women, all with bright dreams for the future, whose stories emerged in the course of researching this book. I imagine many of you know someone like her.

There are lots of possible reasons why Ms. She's professional life took this unexpected direction. Perhaps she was discriminated against so often that she no longer found her goals worth the bother, or maybe she experienced a personal calamity that derailed her plans. On the other hand, maybe, just maybe, the reason lies not in the actions of others, but within Ms. She herself.

Here's what might have happened. Ms. She might have come to actually believe the bias—one so common in her formative years—that says, "Women don't belong in high-level positions in the workplace." This internalization of a bias is tragically common. Several studies, for example, reveal that black children are in danger of buying into the bias that they are unintelligent; white men, that they are less athletic than black men; women, that they are bad at math; and older people, that they are less mentally agile than their younger counterparts.

That's bad news, of course, but it gets worse. When people believe a bias about their group, they then set out to prove it true by making a series of subtle—mostly subconscious—life choices that create what they (because of the bias) expected. The bias, as in the case of Ms. She, becomes a self-fulfilling prophecy.

The "Stereotype Threat": The Enemy of Innovation

Innovation—nothing is more important if we are to succeed in today's competitive marketplace. And nothing compromises innovation more than team members who are, because of a phenomenon known as the "stereotype threat," afraid to speak up with their unique and diverse points of view.

Stereotype threat is the fear of conforming to a negative bias about the group to which we belong. That is, I'm sure you'd agree, a horrible thought. Think, for example, of the stifling effects of being a person over 50 who worries about conforming to the bias "All people over 50 lack creative ideas," or a person under 30 who knows her colleagues are thinking, "All young people aren't experienced enough to have good ideas."

Some people under these circumstances might decide to defy the bias and feel compelled to speak up in order to prove it wrong. Others, understandably, might instead choose to hold themselves back and keep their thoughts to themselves, so as not to risk fulfilling the stereotype. We don't, after all, always come up with our best ideas, and there are days when we are off our game. We are, in short, not always at our best and are, therefore, in constant danger of conforming to the biases that are held against the group to which we belong.

Here is another example of how damaging the stereotype threat can be to both our work and our diversity efforts. The speaker, you need to know, is a white male.

> Some months ago, I was invited to participate in the diversity program at my company. Several colleagues asked me to sit on the Diversity Council and pointed out that having a vice president involved would send a great message to the organization. After initially deciding to jump on board, I heard something that caused me to change my mind. Apparently many people in the organization were expressing views like, "All white males are sexist and racist and don't genuinely buy into creating an inclusive culture." After hearing that, I decided to pass on any involvement with diversity. On a personal level, I just couldn't risk inadvertently saying or doing something that would cause people to label me "just another biased white guy."

These examples make it easy to see how the stereotype threat deprives us of valuable resources in the workplace. Do any of the biases you have identified have the potential of creating a similarly toxic atmosphere?

DOES YOUR BIAS INTERFERE WITH YOUR ABILITY TO SUSTAIN HARMONIOUS TEAMS?

The woman who approached me following the workshop was utterly confused about how to handle what seemed to be a straightforward management challenge. Her confusion surprised me because she had appeared so bright and experienced during the program. I was surprised, that is, until I realized that she was allowing her own personal brand of Guerilla Bias to cloud her judgment. The conversation went something like this.

> I hope I did the right thing. I have several Native American employees who used to be late to work every day. I know they have reliable transportation, so there was no logical reason for them to be so lax. All I could figure out was that it must have something to do with their culture. So I decided to give them some leeway and let them come to work half an hour after everybody else. Now my problem is that the other employees are complaining and want the same flexibility. In my industry, that just isn't going to work. What do I do now?

My response to this woman was a simple, "Why? Why would you allow the Native Americans to come in late when everybody else isn't granted the same privilege?" She answered me by repeating her belief that maybe there was a cultural reason why they couldn't grasp the notion of punctuality. After talking with her a while, I realized that cultural differences were not the problem—her bias was. She was another nice person guilty of the Guerilla Bias that posits that all members of emerging groups have needs so special that they have to be given unique privileges. In this case, that attitude had three negative consequences for her efforts to build harmonious teams:

1. It demeaned the Native Americans by implying that they were unable to measure up to the same standards as their colleagues.
2. It diminished productivity by throwing off the early morning work schedule.
3. It created tension among the team and, according to her, caused the non–Native Americans to look down on their colleagues.

The sad thing about these three losses is that they never would have happened had this manager kept her Guerilla Bias in check and held all her employees to the same strict standard of punctuality.

Having said that, reasonable and respectful accommodation of cultural differences is, of course, a hallmark of a healthy diverse workplace. To help you understand what is reasonable and what is not, here is an example of an adjustment that made sense. It took place at an auto manufacturing plant in Kentucky, where employees of various kinship groups complained about the music being played on the manufacturing floor. In an attempt to accommodate everybody's tastes, management decided to pipe in each group's favorite music on one particular day of the week: country on Monday, urban rock on Tuesday, classical on Wednesday, oldies on Thursday, and reggae on Friday. Sure, some people still complained, but by and large, the situation was nicely resolved: no resentment, no bad feelings, and, most important, no increased bias against any one group that had been given preferential treatment.

DOES YOUR BIAS COMPROMISE THE SUCCESS OF YOUR SALES AND CUSTOMER SERVICE EFFORTS?

Nobody ever suspects him of counting cards. He boldly walks through the doors of casino after casino all "pimped out" in a bright blue suit complete with ruffled shirt. "He bets like wild—raising and lowering from five dollars to five thousand, right under the pit boss's nose. And nobody ever suspects him of anything, because the casinos simply don't believe that a black man can count cards." As Ben Mezrich, author of the nonfiction book *Bringing Down the House,* puts it, the pit bosses' "own racism turns around and bites them."[4]

"Black men can't count cards" is, I'll admit, an unusual bias and the manner in which that bias cost the casinos money no doubt far from your experience. However, for every unusual bias, there are dozens that are commonplace and lie hidden in the minds of your team, just waiting to pop out and cost you business. These biases can take many forms. Perhaps we assume a purchaser doesn't have the money to buy a high-end product, so we fail to cultivate him. Maybe an unconscious bias leaks to the surface causing us to insult a customer who uses a wheelchair by ignoring her and speaking instead to her companion. Perhaps we make broad assumptions about a potential client's negotiation style based solely on his cultural background. The examples go on and on and, to many of you, they would sound painfully familiar. Here is one situation, however, that might not come readily to mind.

Coreen is in pharmaceutical sales. She has lots of experience working with foreign-born doctors and does pretty well in that arena. When it comes to physicians from India, however, she can't seem to succeed. She "knows" they are sexist, however, and figures that's the reason she's having so much difficulty selling to them. As it turns out, it was Coreen's bias, not the doctors' imagined sexism, that was the problem. Because she expected these doctors to treat her badly, she approached them cautiously, restrained her usual charm and warmth, and cut her visits short. It is no surprise that, as the number of Indian physicians increased in her territory, Coreen's sales figures declined.

As her commission check began to shrink, Coreen had to face the fact that she had allowed her bias to distract her from one of the first things she had learned when joining the company: the importance of taking time to assess the unique needs and personality of your customer. Had she paid attention to her individual customer rather than her bias, she might just have salvaged thousands of dollars in lost revenue.

DOES YOUR BIAS PUT YOUR ORGANIZATION AT RISK FOR LITIGATION?

Racist jokes, gay bashing, sexual harassment, and litigation. I bet I have your attention now. Litigation is the worst nightmare of every organization, every manager, and every CEO. Tragically, this particular nightmare has a way of coming true with alarming regularity. Sometimes the waking dream is filled with contemptible characters who tell racist jokes, denigrate gay people, or make sleazy comments to female subordinates. Other times, and this is the real worry, the act that results in litigation is of the Guerilla Bias variety; no sleazy and easily identifiable characters are in sight.

I doubt, for example, that the manager who inspired Meg's race discrimination suit was particularly sleazy; he was probably even "nice." Because he was so nice, he couldn't bring himself to tell her that she was doing a bad job. He was, you see, afraid that Meg would be offended by his comments. Eventually, Meg's performance became so bad that, despite his fear of her reaction, he fired her. This wouldn't, of course, have been a problem had he given Meg some warning—along with the information she needed in order to improve. Unfortunately, he didn't give her these things. What he did give her was clear grounds for a discrimination suit, which, by the way, Meg ultimately won.

Like Meg's manager, most frontline sales associates and customer contact staff are basically nice people, but being nice is never a defense against litigation. Here's how one nice person's bias cost her hotel chain thousands of dollars in legal fees.

It took the man three hours to get drunk and disorderly at the hotel bar, but only a few minutes to turn one small lie into a discrimination suit. Julio was so drunk that it amazed everyone that he was able to find his way to the reception desk and ask for a room, but he did and that's when the trouble began. Realizing she couldn't rent to Julio because of his condition, the clerk pretended to check the computer then turned to him and lied: "I'm sorry, sir, there are no rooms available; I'm afraid I'll have to ask you to leave."

Upon hearing the bad news, Julio uttered a few well-used obscenities and staggered away, only to collapse in a nearby chair. Within a few minutes, a white couple approached the desk, asked if there were any vacancies, and received the key to a room on the 14th floor. Julio overheard this exchange and, even in his bleary state, understood its significance. Once he sobered up, Julio didn't take long to find a lawyer and sue for discrimination.

When later asked why she didn't tell Julio the truth, the clerk said she didn't want him to think she was discriminating against Latinos. "If he had been white, I probably would have just told him we don't rent to people who are drunk and sent him on his way." Nobody is saying we ought to call even one rowdy customer a drunk, but in some ways it would have been better—and even, oddly, more respectful—than treating Julio as if he were incapable of handling the truth. The irony is that the clerk's dishonesty created exactly what she was trying to prevent: expensive litigation and even more expensive bad publicity.

CHAPTER SUMMARY

- The biases that most deserve our attention are those that cause the greatest damage in terms of hurt feelings, ruined relationships, and compromised productivity.
- Biases interfere with appropriate hiring decisions by negating our ability to evaluate applicants accurately.
- Biases threaten the retention of quality employees in many ways, including when they distort our perceptions of what individuals of diverse backgrounds have to offer. These distortions may be because of negative biases regarding their abilities or because of positive or Guerilla Biases.
- Biases interfere with individual productivity and success by causing us to hold team members to a low standard of performance, preventing us from providing appropriate feedback, and causing us to act on our biases in such a way that they become self-fulfilling prophecies.
- The internalization of biases and the fear of inadvertently confirming a bias (stereotype threat) are stifling to both the expression of innovative ideas and workplace effectiveness.
- Guerilla Biases interfere with the harmony of diverse teams when they seduce us into giving unreasonable preferential treatment to particular groups.
- Biases interfere with successful sales and customer service when they cause us to misinterpret the buying power, needs, or attitudes of clients and the public.
- Biases can result in litigation, not only when they are blatant and negative, but also when they masquerade as good intentions and kindly acts.

6

STEP THREE: IDENTIFY THE SECONDARY GAINS OF YOUR BIASES

CHAPTER FOCUS QUESTION

What am I gaining by holding onto my biases?

In the aftermath of September 11, 2001, Arab-Americans were the unhappy targets of biased people of all stripes. I met one of these targets on September 30 of that fateful year. I don't remember his name, but I do remember his pain and the glimpse I had of the rage that lurked just below his courteous demeanor. He was a Lebanese cabdriver, and he was frustrated and more than a little frightened at how badly some of his passengers had treated him since the World Trade Center attacks.

Most of those who hurt this man so deeply were merely abrupt or cold or sat stiffly in the backseat with frightened looks in their eyes. One woman, however, opened the cab door, took in the driver's Semitic features and Arab accent, and started yelling, "You are all a bunch of terrorists. I wouldn't ride with someone like you. Why don't you go home and leave our country alone?" The driver admitted he lost his temper and lobbed obscenities at the back of the would-be passenger as she scurried away in search of a driver with a lighter complexion.

As he told his story, I could tell the man was ashamed of his reaction. It was obvious that those obscenities had sprung from a need to hide the hurt caused by the passenger's refusal to see him for what he was: an immigrant who loved America and had worked hard to make a living in what he firmly believed was the greatest nation on earth.

The passenger had a bias ("You are all a bunch of terrorists") that was both dangerous and, except for how much it upset everybody in its path, seemingly pointless. It didn't make her any happier and certainly didn't help her form more fulfilling relationships. So why did she persist in believing as she did?

The answer lies in the truism of the human mind that most otherwise unproductive attitudes and behaviors carry within them what is called a "secondary gain." Sometimes that gain feels, at least temporarily, good. Take chronic lateness, for example. We all know that tardiness is not a good thing; it irritates people, makes life more stressful, and all-around is a behavior that doesn't have much to say for itself. So why do some people make a habit of being late? They must get something out of it. They must get a secondary gain, or they wouldn't keep it up.

In the case of lateness, those secondary gains include attention (everyone is talking about us before we arrive and commenting on our arrival once we appear), a feeling of power over those who are waiting (they can't start without us), and the titillation of living just a little bit on the edge. Of course, none of those gains is worth the price we pay by creating a reputation of being unreliable and raising the ire of those we have inconvenienced. But, until we become aware of those secondary gains and measure them against the cost of being chronically late, the odds of our getting up a little earlier, planning ahead more carefully, or getting directions before heading out are slim.

Reader Exploration Point: Think about a bad habit you may have. Perhaps it is procrastination, eating too much, not picking up after yourself, or any other behavior that isn't a good idea, but that you just can't seem to stop. What secondary gain do you get out of that behavior?

The secondary gain that our frightened taxi fare got from her inflexible belief that all people from the Middle East are terrorists was the illusion that she could predict how they would behave. That illusion, in turn, made her feel marginally more secure in her increasingly insecure world.

Every bias has a secondary gain attached to it. Some of those gains are real; others are merely illusions. In every case, however, the gain is not worth all the trouble the bias causes. Once we realize that, we move one step closer to being willing to let the bias go.

Your task in this chapter is to figure out the perks that you feel accompany the biases you have identified in yourself. To help you do this, the chapter is divided into several sections, each of which discusses a possible secondary gain.

- The Power to Predict the Future—Bias as Magical Thinking
- Protection from Diminished Status
- Protection from Loss
- Protection from Emotional Pain
- An Excuse to Avoid Discomfort

SECONDARY GAIN: THE POWER TO PREDICT THE FUTURE—BIAS AS MAGICAL THINKING

Fear, magic, and bias—all are part of the human condition and all are connected. What do fear and magic have to do with bias? As you'll soon see, bias is an integral part of this chain and is, in fact, a type of magical thinking.

By the way, do you believe in magic? I imagine your initial response to that question is no. What if I asked the question slightly differently? Do you practice any superstitious rituals? It might be that you use a "magical" pen to complete a job application. Perhaps you feel the irrepressible urge to knock on wood when you speak of something good in your life. Or, if you are a golfer, maybe you are compelled to tap the club head on the ground before driving or to fondle those lucky tees in your left pants pocket. Maybe you don't *really* believe in the ritual; maybe it is little more than an itch you seem compelled to scratch, despite your better judgment.

But that counts too—you do scratch the itch and that makes you at least a little bit of a believer.

If you are still unconvinced that you are superstitious, let me ask you another question: Have you recently made a wish on a birthday candle? If the answer is yes—and 90 percent of the time it is—here's a follow-up question: What is the cardinal rule of making that wish come true?

I can practically hear your answer in my head: "You never tell anyone the wish." Funny how we all, despite our cultural differences, know the answer to that question. Here's yet another question. Since we never tell the wish, what is there to stop us from standing in front of that cake and thinking something like, "This is just a silly superstition. I'm not going to really make a wish. I'll just pretend to do so for the sake of the children"? The truth is, there is nothing to stop us from faking the wish, but we don't. We go ahead and, I would wager, very carefully consider our options. Speaking strictly for me, I put a lot of thought into my wish, just in case. After all, you never know . . .

Let's face it, most human beings are a bit superstitious. We, especially in times of stress, indulge in magical thinking. That is because all magical belief grows from something we share: fear. Human beings are fundamentally afraid. We are afraid of death, we are afraid of physical pain, and we are even afraid of being afraid. It is this fear that animates—and propels—magical thinking and magic's first cousin, bias.

Magic, you see, serves to relieve fear. It does this by leading us to believe we can influence and predict things that, in reality, are out of our control and out of our sphere of knowledge. That is exactly the same function that bias serves. It supplies us with the illusion that we know what people are like and that we know what they will do in the future.

Bias, also like magic, isn't very good at its job. Sure, every once in a while someone comes along who happens to conform to our bias—after all, these inflexible beliefs came from somewhere, people do exist who have the characteristics that inhabit our bias. And, sure, once in a while your birthday wish coincidentally comes true. But, most of the time, both wishes and biases provide only the illusion of success. Just as tossing a coin in a fountain leaves us with an initial feeling of optimism, only to let us down when the wish fails to come true, a bias at first make us feel more secure, only to create more anxiety when its inaccuracies are exposed.

SECONDARY GAIN: PROTECTION FROM DIMINISHED STATUS

Even the horrific bias that early European settlers had against the native populations of the New World was paired with a secondary gain. That gain was protection of the Europeans' belief in their status as civilized human beings. Isolated and stranded in an unfamiliar environment, far from the lace curtains and polished pewter of which they were so fond, the Europeans feared they might slide down a muddy slope and land in a heap beside what they perceived to be the uncivilized inhabitants of "their" new land.

To reassure themselves that they were still socially refined, the settlers needed to create a sharp contrast between themselves and their Native American neighbors. They did this by cultivating the illusion that Native Americans were profoundly and, most telling, "naturally" barbaric. This bias served in their minds to utterly distinguish the "them" from the "us" and eliminate any danger of the "civilized" group being mistaken for the "savage" one.

More than 300 years later, Marie, a Mexican-born nurse-practitioner, had a similar concern. She complained of constantly being assigned to care for, as she put it, "those dirty, uneducated Mexican immigrants." As it turns out, her bias came directly from the fear that her contact with these patients would somehow pull her back down into a status and lifestyle she had come to find repulsive. To relieve this fear, Marie manufactured the bias that these patients were in possession of remarkably few redeeming virtues and were irrevocably beneath her in terms of their position in the social stratum.

One would think that Marie's personal experience with the pain of low status would beget compassion for others. Unfortunately, the opposite is often true. In fact, bias is one way in which we relieve our insecurities; it enables us to look down on others from a precarious perch of imagined superiority.

SECONDARY GAIN: PROTECTION FROM LOSS

Fear of losing something we believe to be rightfully ours is one of the most common reasons for the development of a bias. This explains why biases increase in times of economic slowdown and why it is then that we begin to hear a medley of mantras about how "those people" are "taking all the jobs," "getting preferential treatment," and "taking advantage of the situation." Yale psychologists Carl Hovland and Robert Sears, working in the 1920s and 1930s, found that when cotton prices in the South went down, the number of lynchings went up.[1] Legend or myth or fact—it's hard to tell from this distance—tells us that when the Roman Empire was crumbling, Christians were more frequently fed to lions. True or not, we do know that this penchant for using bias as a way to protect our supply of limited resources has been with humankind from the beginning.

Nan, a bank manager in Southern California, provides us with a modern example of how this process works.

> I had been at the branch for several years, and we always had good employees. That is until I hired Akbar, a young man who had emigrated from Iran. At first everything was fine, but then Akbar started acting strangely, staying late, and being generally uncommunicative. One Monday morning, he failed to show up. We soon realized that Akbar was gone, along with thousands of dollars of our customers' deposits.
>
> When my regional supervisor found out what happened, he was furious and blamed me for not having made a better hiring decision. It even looked, for a while, like I would lose my job. To this day, I have trouble objectively evaluating any Iranian applicant. I'm trying, but I keep thinking they will all be like Akbar, and I sure don't want my job to be on the line again.

The truth is that Nan's bias—"All Iranians are thieves"—did temporarily benefit her by making her feel more secure about her job. As long as she clung to that bias, she was in no danger of hiring another one of "them" and having another one of "them" steal from the bank. Therefore, she was in no danger of being fired.

Ultimately, however, there is a very high price to pay for this ridiculous exercise in inflexible belief. If Nan sticks by her bias and continues to refuse to hire Iranian employees, she and her organization are at risk on two fronts. First, and most obviously, they are at risk of being sued for discrimination—and the complaint would be both legally and morally valid. Second, and this is more a certainty than a risk, they will miss out on the many fine employees that no doubt are to be found in the local Iranian community.

SECONDARY GAIN: PROTECTION FROM EMOTIONAL PAIN

Mark has a bias. He believes that all fully abled (or, as he is fond of saying with a nod toward Father Time, temporarily abled) people look down on him and others with disabilities. This inflexible generality—that all members of a given group are biased—is perhaps the only prejudice that is actually tolerated in the workplace. That toleration is unfortunate because by putting up with the personal fiction that "all men are sexist" or that "all white people are racist," or, as in Mark's case, "all fully abled people look down on people with disabilities," we promote the notion that some biases are acceptable and others are not; nothing could be further from the truth.

Prejudices like Mark's—I'll clumsily call it the "bias bias"—are usually triggered by a desire to protect oneself from a repetition of emotional pain. From Mark's point of view, as destructive as his bias is, it does keep him from being caught off guard next time he is treated like a child or ignored as if he, and his wheelchair, were invisible. Mark, you see, is a paraplegic who for years has been patronized by strangers. Because of these experiences, he has developed a bias against anyone who offers him assistance. The bias is so bad that at even the simplest offer of kindness, he is apt to bristle and snap, "I am perfectly capable of taking care of myself." Sadly, Mark has become just as biased as that minority of people who assume that "all people with disabilities are to be patronized and pitied."

Jesse, a 30-year-old recent immigrant from Guatemala, possesses an equally strong desire to protect himself from emotional pain and thus has developed a bias that is as effective as Mark's at shielding him from unexpected blows. Jesse has had a truly rough time of it. He has been laughed at by native-born Americans for his limited English, beaten by a gang of white supremacists, and repeatedly passed over for promotions, all due to his heritage. Because of these experiences, it is understandable—although misguided—that Jesse now holds the bias that "all white people are racist" and sees bigotry everywhere, all the time, in every white person he meets. His own prejudice leads him to interpret the gray areas of each word and action as a sure sign of racism against him and his fellow Latinos. In that sense, his bias has temporarily benefited him, by shielding him from any surprises. It has also cost him dearly in lost friendships, hurt feelings, and missed opportunities.

SECONDARY GAIN: AN EXCUSE TO AVOID DISCOMFORT

The culprit in this section is our old nemesis and the nice person's bias of choice, Guerilla Bias. As you recall, this brand of bias is based on the premise that all members of certain groups need special treatment. This bias is frequently disguised behind kind thoughts such as, "I don't want to hurt his feelings," "I don't want to make anyone upset," or, my personal favorite, "I wouldn't want to risk offending anybody." Because Guerilla Bias is so hard to detect, you would think that the secondary gains it provides would be equally difficult to determine. In fact, at least one of those gains is pretty obvious: Guerilla Bias reinforces our view of ourselves as nice people. A second alleged benefit is a little tougher to spot.

> *Guerilla Bias provides an excuse to stay away from people around whom we feel uncomfortable.*

Take a look at these examples. Do either of them sound or feel familiar?

The Waiter and the Wheelchair
- *Behavior:* A waiter ignores the woman with cerebral palsy and asks her male companion what she would like to eat.
- *Alleged reason for the behavior:* "This poor woman has enough problems. I don't want to embarrass her by making her talk. I know she has difficulty speaking clearly." (Guerilla Bias: "People with disabilities are not really like the rest of us; they are emotionally fragile and need special treatment.")

- *Real reason for the behavior:* The waiter is uncomfortable with people with disabilities. He is the one who is embarrassed and wants to avoid the conversation. Certainly it is possible that the woman will have difficulty speaking, but it is she and her companion, not a stranger, who should decide how to handle the situation.
- *Excuse provided by his Guerilla Bias:* His bias temporarily benefited the waiter by giving him an excuse ("I want to be nice") to avoid talking directly to the woman.

The Manager and the Immigrant

- *Behavior:* A manager makes an effort not to sit next to her newly hired Russian-born account executive at the company banquet.
- *Alleged reason for the behavior:* "If I sit next to him, I know he will feel obligated to speak with me because I am his boss. I'm sure he'll be embarrassed because of his accent. It would be kinder not to put him in that position." (Guerilla Bias: "People who aren't skilled at speaking English are all easily embarrassed and need to be treated with kid gloves.")
- *Real reason for the behavior:* The manager is afraid she won't understand the man; it is she, not the account executive, who is worried about being embarrassed and uncomfortable.
- *Excuse provided by her Guerilla Bias:* Her bias temporarily benefited the manager by giving her an excuse not to engage the account executive in conversation and, thereby, to avoid the possibility of being embarrassed by not understanding him.

There is a chance, of course, that what these contributors are struggling to avoid—discomfort, embarrassment, or misunderstanding—could come to pass and, let's face it, one way to minimize that risk is to avoid contact. The problem, however, is, as we saw in Chapter 5, that we pay a painfully high price for this tenuous feeling of security.

CONCLUSION: A CAUTIONARY NOTE

This is the point in the Vision Renewal Process where you just might be tempted to close this book and abruptly terminate your journey toward bias reduction. Why wouldn't you? Earlier you were reassured that biases don't make you a bad person; in this chapter, you were shown that biases can, in some ways, offer some temporary gain. Taking all this into consideration, you'd have every right to ask, "Why not wrap it up right here?" The reason to continue with the process is that the benefits you have identified in this chapter are tenuous at best and, in any case, could not possibly be worth the high price you pay for indulging in your biases.

CHAPTER SUMMARY:

- Like any other negative attitude, biases bring a slight and illusory secondary gain. If we are to rid ourselves of bias, we need to identify that gain and make the decision that it is not worth the damage that our biases cause.
- Most biases are like magical thinking in that they provide the illusion that we can predict what people will be like and what they will do in the future.
- Some biases delude us into thinking that we are, and deserve to be, of higher status than other groups.
- Biases provide us with the temporary benefit of protection from the loss of something we feel is rightfully ours.
- Biases prevent the repetition of emotional pain. This is particularly true of the "bias bias," which holds that certain kinship groups are inevitably biased against others.
- Guerilla Bias allows us to feel better about staying away from people around whom we are uncomfortable.

CHAPTER

7

STEP FOUR: DISSECT YOUR BIASES

CHAPTER FOCUS QUESTION

How can I examine my biases to weaken their foundation?

Lynn remembers it clearly (sort of). It has happened many, many times (but she can't exactly remember when). (Almost) every time she was teamed with one of "them," they were so lazy she had to do all the work (mostly). Besides, she heard from her friend that the ones he worked with were that way, too.

Vague memories, questionable experiences, and rumors—not exactly what I would call reliable sources of information. Lynn obviously needs to undergo the next step in the Vision Renewal Process. Like most of us, she must dissect her biases to show how unreliable they are. Although this stage of the process can be fun, especially if you enjoy thinking analytically, it can also be a little embarrassing when we discover the fragile foundation on which most of our biases are built.

Step Four uses inquiry, as anthropologist Jennifer James puts it, to "move our responses to others out of our guts and into our minds."[1] This inquiry will take the form of three questions, each of which, if answered honestly, will reveal the faulty logic behind your biases.

QUESTION 1: WHERE DID YOU LEARN YOUR BIAS AND UNDER WHAT CIRCUMSTANCES?

"Tribal Leaders" as Sources of Bias

Many of us grew up in homes that were veritable petri dishes of the bias virus. We lived each moment watching, listening, and experiencing in an atmosphere infected with biased messages and subtle (or not-so-subtle) examples of distorted vision. It may not be fashionable these days to blame parents for our faulty thinking, but when it comes to bias, we must lay the responsibility firmly in Mom and Dad's overburdened laps.

Parents are the most powerful people we know during our formative years. They are our tribal leaders and because they are the primary force that guides us, we believe what they say. If parents are open-minded (read unafraid), that is great. Children of open-minded parents learn to be in the moment and evaluate each person as she comes along; they have no psychological need to divine the nature or intentions of individuals according to the group to which they belong. If, on the other hand, our parents are carriers of bias, we become infected not only with the specific biases that they hold, but also with the notion that biased thinking in general is an effective approach to solving life's problems.

Of all the biases our parents teach us, it is the subtle ones that are the most insidious. If you have a parent who is blatantly biased, whose idea, for example, of a good time on a Saturday night is to burn a cross on someone's lawn, at least the message is clear. Because the bias is obvious, we—the children—can easily name it, dispute it, and eliminate it from our thinking.

On the other hand, most parents provide a gentler primer for bias that is, paradoxically, harder to unlearn. Take my friend Carol, for example. Carol has only the vaguest memory of the subtly racist attitudes her black father voiced about the white friends she brought home. As such, she was unaware, until her late 20s, of the bias against whites with which she was infected. Comments like, "I'd be happier if you would find friends who are more like us," or, "Heather seems nice enough, but she is white, after all," left Carol with the subtle message that friendship with "those" white people is just not a good idea.

Lee is another example. His Guerilla Biased view that people with disabilities are emotionally fragile grew from the embarrassment he glimpsed in his mother's face anytime he, as a child, would point to someone with a disability and ask, in less-than-discrete tones, why they were rolling in a chair, or why they had a white cane, or, worst of all why their face looked "funny." Her reaction was subtle, but the message loud and clear: "Don't call attention to 'handicapped people'; they are too damaged to handle it."

The most potent of bias-creating messages are, not only subtle, but ambiguous or even contradictory. My father was a master at, if not subtlety, certainly contradiction. He and my mother were what I call "ambivalent racists." As a result of having lived through a wide variety of experiences and mixed cultural messages, their thinking was precariously balanced between the mores of 1930s white America and 1960s semi-enlightenment. My father was, therefore, in some ways wise and in other ways ignorant—a state that caused him to deliver mixed messages to my impressionable mind.

Here's just one example of how ambiguous my father's diversity message was. For some time, when he was first in Hollywood struggling to establish his career, he stood on a skid row street corner, with men of all races and ethnicities, hoping for any manual labor that might come along. Never during this period did a word of bias, hatred, or fear come out of his mouth toward his fellow laborers. On the other hand, years later when I was the victim of an armed robbery, his first question was, "Were they black?" This question contradicted my father's obvious respect for his skid row chums. Because the message I received was inconsistent, it was difficult to refute, difficult to cleanly label as "bigotry," and, therefore, hard to target for extinction.

Reader Exploration Point: Think back to your childhood and try to recall a subtle or mixed message of bias that might have been imparted to you by your parents. What is your first memory of having heard that message? Do you think that message affected your thinking today?

The Media as a Source of Bias

Television, radio, the Web, and newspapers are, of course, abundant sources of bias. From pictures of chanting Muslims during the news hour

Workplace Application:
How to Counteract Media-created Bias

When negative events occur that are highly publicized in the media, there is real danger of new biases being created or old ones rekindled. The way to counter the effect of such coverage is to facilitate meetings at which deliberate, immediate, and systematic dialogue about the event can take place.

The Purpose: To put the event in perspective, reduce rumor, and diffuse emotions that can result in bias and inappropriate workplace behavior.

Preparation: As much as possible, the facilitator of the meeting should research facts about the event: Who was really involved? What is proved as fact, and what is only speculation? What rumors are circulating about this event?

Suggested Agenda Items:

1. Give participants the opportunity to talk about their perceptions of the event.
2. Encourage individuals to share their emotional reactions to the event. This, of course, needs to be done within the boundaries of respectful language.
3. Clarify any media distortions of the event with particular emphasis on unconfirmed or erroneous rumors.
4. Provide guidance on how to discuss the event with others in the workplace. (See Part Three of this book.)

to casting choices that perpetuate positive and negative stereotypes, none of us can escape the images that the media supplies.

The media is a particularly dangerous producer of bias because of its penchant for exaggerating reality. It presents isolated incidents as trends, turns cultural characteristics into caricatures, and worst of all, bombards us with inflated dangers. Unless the threat is an earthquake or hurricane, these dangers are inevitably linked to some group of human beings. Inevitably, too, the actions of these groups—whether they are inner-city youths or Muslims or fundamentalist Christians—are depicted in the most brilliant colors. It is, of course, both unethical and unwise to generalize, but, (as a broad statement) many in the media feel that there is no story unless there is drama. And what is more dramatic than violence and threat? It is often said of the media, "If it bleeds, it reads."

It is not, however, only negative biases that the media creates and perpetuates. Print, broadcast, and electronic media are equally guilty of indoctrinating the culture into inflexible beliefs that contain positive characteristics such as "all men are strong," "all older people are wise," "all gay men are fashion conscious," and, that old favorite, "all black people have rhythm." These positive biases, as we have seen, can interfere as readily as the negative ones with our ability to see people accurately.

Reader Exploration Point: Here is a way to get in touch with the positive biases you may have picked up from the media. Think of three television shows that you watch or have watched regularly. They can be from any period in your life. List the positive images depicted in these shows and the groups they are supposed to reflect. How have these images impacted your view of these groups today?

Experience as a Source of Bias

Of all the ways we learn bias, you would think that experience would be the most reliable. After all, we were there, we lived it, and we know what happened. Well, maybe and maybe not. For one thing, any experience with one individual, or even 10 individuals, says nothing about other members of that kinship group. In addition, unless an experience is well rounded and repeated, it tells us little even about the person actually encountered. That is because . . .

A given experience may not mean what we think it does.

One reason for this distortion is that most experiences that give rise to bias are brief and one-dimensional. Each is like a snapshot taken from one angle only, and that angle is, by physical necessity, from the perspective of the person holding the camera. The other side of the subject and the subtleties of shading and dimension that would accurately reflect her appearance are never recorded. If you don't believe me, think of the number of times you have reacted to a photo of yourself by asking, often with considerable trepidation, "That doesn't really look like me, does it?"

Another reason brief encounters are unreliable is that they are distorted by the emotions we bring to them—emotions that mean we can't trust what our senses are telling us. Fear, guilt, anxiety, and myriad other feelings can leave us thinking that something happened differently than it did.

I will use a bias with which I still struggle to illustrate this point. That bias is not the subtle or unconscious kind with which this book is concerned; it is the type that stands bravely in front of me distorting my view of many people I meet. That bias reads, "All black men are potentially dangerous in some way."

Like many such biases, this one was generated and regenerated by multiple sources. The ambivalent racist parents I mentioned earlier were one source and the media, with its perpetual depiction of black youths as drug-crazed gangsters, was another. In terms of experience, there wasn't much, but what there was, was fraught with emotion.

The setting of one of those experiences was a gas station in an upscale Southern California neighborhood. It being in the dark days before cell phones, I had pulled in to make an urgent call at the pay phone. Knowing that I would not be long, I left the car in a spot clearly marked No Parking. Just as I was about to dial the number, a young black man who worked for the station walked up, stood within what felt like six inches of my face, looked me straight in the eye with an intensity I will never forget, and demanded that I move the car.

I know, I know, right about now you're thinking, "No wonder she was upset; that's pretty scary." Well, sort of. Yes, my perception at that time was that the attendant was angry and about to lose control. However, when I look back on the incident, I realize that my own emotion just might have played more than a small part in how I perceived that event and the players in it.

What I haven't told you yet is that I was pretty agitated myself when I pulled into that gas station. There had been a mishap at the university, and I was rushing to a colleague's house to see if we could resolve the problem. I suspect that anyone who stood in my way that stressful afternoon would

Workplace Application: The Power of Images

The images that surround us have the power to create, sustain, and, if handled properly, reduce both conscious and unconscious bias. Because of this power, we need to be alert to how we depict people in our publications, advertisements, and Web sites. Here are some suggestions for effective bias-reducing imagery. The options are almost limitless and depend on your corporate culture, the biases found in your organization, and your diversity goals.

1. To reduce biases against people with disabilities, you might depict a person with a visible disability in a position of influence or performing a task that others might erroneously believe would be impossible for the individual.

2. In an effort to reduce bias by creating an awareness of shared kinship groups, you might depict people who are visibly different sharing an activity, interest, or project. The image of people of diverse backgrounds performing an activity together is more effective at reducing bias than one in which they are shown individually.

3. To reduce stereotypes about the skills and interests of particular groups, you might depict those groups in "counter bias" positions. You could, for example, depict a person of Asian background in a people management position and a person of another group at the computer.

4. If your organization is challenged with reducing biases that limit the upward mobility of certain groups, you might depict people from these groups in positions of obvious authority.

5. To fight what has been called "lookism," you might depict a person who is considered overweight in a position of authority and responsibility.

have seemed hostile. It is very possible that my own emotions influenced my evaluation of a person who was just doing his job. In either case, whether this man was indeed threatening or my senses misled me, I experienced and remembered the incident as negative and frightening.

Tragically, it is negative events like this, be they real or imagined, that have the power to create the most firmly held biases. The reason for this is that anything negative, if taken to its logical conclusion, threatens our survival and, therefore, gives rise to strong emotions. As pioneering psychologist Gordon Allport puts it, "Intense emotional feelings have a property of acting like sponges. Ideas, engulfed by an overpowering emotion, are more likely to conform to the emotion than to objective evidence."[2] Allport's "ideas" are our biases.

If we add to this what researchers call "terror management theory," we have a real mess. Terror management theory suggests that fear causes us to turn to those whom we think of as "our own" and reject those who are outside our group.[3] Because of this distancing, not only do we become afraid of those who are not "us," we also begin to exaggerate the differences between the two groups.

Picture, for example, a five-week-old puppy named Bliss tentatively venturing out from her mother. Startled by the hiss of a cat, the dog whirls around and scurries back to the warmth of its pile of littermates—her own version of a human kinship group. That puppy, particularly if it is at a formative period in its social development, is in danger of forever assuming, because of the intensity of that emotion, that "all cats are dangerous" and, to make matters worse, of having an exaggerated idea of how different cats are from dogs. Bliss the puppy, in essence, becomes biased.

Geraldo probably wouldn't want to hear it, but he is just like that puppy. Because of one frightening experience with one passenger, this San Antonio cabdriver will not give rides to young black men. And Ron, who always thought of himself as a tolerant sort, refuses to hire a female assistant because of the false sexual harassment charges the last one brought against him. Both men have allowed the emotion they experienced on one occasion to color their perception of an entire population of people.

There is still one more reason that negative and emotional events so economically create bias: They, almost by definition, involve some element of drama and danger. Let's face it, human beings are fascinated with drama. Why else would the media be so successful when it reports and exaggerates stories of violence and hatred? Why else do so many of us like scary movies or participate in sports that are just a little bit risky. We have to face it, most of us like the illusion or reality of a little danger in our lives.

Anthropologist Jennifer James addresses this issue when she says that we "love the feeling of being in battle, [we are] hunters and warriors at heart." Danger, she argues, gives us an adrenaline rush and the opportunity to prove our cunning and our strength.[4] It is the craving for this rush that tempts us to transform a negative encounter into a belief in an ongoing threat; we do this by adopting a negative bias about the group involved. Negative bias becomes, therefore, a device that allows us to believe we are still conquering the frontier, girding for battle, or, at the very least, being just a little bit braver than our daily routines allow us to demonstrate.

Reader Exploration Point: Pick one of the biases you have identified and try to remember how you learned it. Was it from someone you respected or from a person who clearly had distorted views of other people? Was it from the media? Did it grow from one emotionally charged experience?

QUESTION 2: HOW MANY PEOPLE HAVE YOU ACTUALLY MET WHO CONFORM TO YOUR BIAS?

Caution! The phrase "actually met" does not include media images, rumor, what other people say they know; all that counts here are personal encounters between members of the group in question and you. You'll notice that I have deliberately said *encounters* not *encounter.* Too often biases grow out of one experience with one person or, at most, with one small group of people.

On top of that, even if a negative situation is encountered repeatedly, the percentage of any kinship group with which you have direct experience will *still* be absurdly small. Ask yourself, "How many members of this group have I actually met who have this characteristic?"

For Hannah, that number was three. Hannah bears the burden of believing that "all men are sexist." She believes this because she has had three sexist bosses in her 25-year career. Now let's see if we can figure this out. There are about 120,000,000 men in the United States of the age that might have been Hannah's boss. Hannah knows three who are sexist. This means that in her direct experience—which is the only experience she can count on and, as we saw, even that might be faulty—she knows for sure that .000003 percent of American men are sexist. I don't know about you, but I can't even grasp how small a percentage that is. My accountant tells me it is something like three millionths of one percent, hardly a statistic on which to base your opinion of an entire population of people.

QUESTION 3: HAVE YOU EVER MET A MEMBER OF YOUR TARGET GROUP WHO DOES NOT CONFORM TO YOUR BIAS?

I am reminded of a young woman named Rose who told me with complete confidence that "all Mexicans are destructive." That misguided belief grew out of one horrifying night when two Mexican immigrant teen-agers tried to break into her house. When the boys found they couldn't get in, they became furious and destroyed her front fence. Rose was alone, her phone was disconnected, and she was, understandably, terrified.

After she told me this story, I asked if she knew any Mexicans who weren't destructive. She looked at me as if that were the stupidest question she had ever heard and said, "Oh, yes, I live in a mostly Mexican community and all my neighbors are wonderful people." When I pointed out the inconsistency between "All Mexicans are destructive" and her feelings about her neighbors, it was obviously a revelation to her. Under the bright light of logic, you could almost see her bias melt away. Sadly, the intensity of her negative experience with the two boys had clouded her memory of the good people around whom she had built her life.

CHAPTER SUMMARY

- Examining the source of a bias is a powerful tool for weakening its influence. This is because that source is usually unreliable.
- Parents are effective teachers of bias. Although the blatant prejudices we learn as children are dangerous, it is the subtle and ambiguous messages of bias that, because of how hard they are to see, are the most difficult to dislodge.

- The media creates and perpetuates both positive and negative biases.
- Experience may seem a reliable source of bias, but, in fact, it is not. This is because experiences with any member of a group are one-dimensional and often distorted by emotion.
- The foundation of a bias can be weakened by examining how many people we actually know who conform to the bias. It is also helpful to look at past encounters to see whom we have met whose characteristics run counter to our biased belief.

STEP FIVE: IDENTIFY COMMON KINSHIP GROUPS

CHAPTER FOCUS QUESTION

How can I redefine my kinship groups in order to minimize my biases?

Even Alice was amazed as she watched herself reach out and sweep the contents off the top of the receptionist's desk. College educated, bright, and usually reserved, Alice had been hired over the phone for a long-sought-after position. It's a common tale, you've heard it or lived it before. She showed up at the office only to see the receptionist's face blanch and watch as she scurried away into a nearby office. The receptionist returned a few minutes later, accompanied in her wake by the sound of a door slamming and the strains of her boss's voice yelling, "Get her out of here. How could you be so stupid? You know we don't hire colored people."

It was futile for the receptionist to make excuses. Alice knew what had happened. It had happened before—and before, and before. Alice was tired, and she lost control. She could no longer restrain her frustration and anger. Now a manager at a large West Coast bank, Alice tells the story without pride but with a certain understandable justification.

Prue, 78 years old and the wife of a retired oil executive, never swept anything off anyone's desk. Maybe it would have done her some good if she had, though, for you can still hear the pain 60 years after her disappointment. Prue speaks of her lofty professional aspirations when she graduated, at the top of her MBA class, from the University of Texas. She soon found, however, that despite the temporary progress made by women during World War II, the oil business had no interest in hiring a professional female in 1948. By contrast, her husband, who admits his grades were "just OK," stepped easily into his first job and rose rapidly to the top of his profession.

Prue has regrets. She does not regret the family she raised nor the support she gave her husband through the years; she does regret, and grieves over, the career that never was.

Alice and Prue are different women. One is black, one white; one was raised in California, one in Texas. But they share the same frustration, a frustration caused by bias and discrimination. In that sense, they are members of the same kinship group. No longer separated by race, age, or geography, their shared experience, if recognized, would broaden for each a previously narrow sense of "usness" to include each other.

The next step in the Vision Renewal Process is to do what Alice and Prue might have done: redefine kinship groups so that they include those toward whom we hold a bias. This chapter contains five strategies designed to help each of us accomplish this important goal.

1. Keep What We Share Top-of-Mind
2. Practice Skills for Achieving Empathy
3. Seek Contact with Those Who Are Different from You
4. Create Workplace Opportunities for Cross-group Contact
5. Create and Emphasize Shared Goals

First, however, we'll examine how and why redefining our notion of the group to which we belong automatically diminishes bias.

HOW SHARING A KINSHIP GROUP REDUCES BIAS

As we saw in the introduction to this book, a kinship group is "any population that shares a self- or externally ascribed characteristic that sets it apart from others." This characteristic might be a disability, race, hobby, gender, age, or any other of dozens of human dimensions. The virtue in the concept of a kinship group is that it allows each of us to belong to many groups at once, depending on the characteristic on which we focus. It also—and this is the best part—enables us to broaden our group to include many populations that we previously thought of as different from ourselves.

Here is one of the many advantages of sharing a kinship group:

Once you identify yourself with a particular population, members of that group are transformed in your mind from "them" to "us."

An Asian-American might, for example, initially see her Latino colleague only in terms of how different he is from her: Latino, not Asian; man, not woman. If, however, she has the opportunity to know him better, she very likely will begin to see him as a variety of things, not all of which are "different." Perhaps she runs into him at the grocery store and discovers that, like her, he is a gourmet cook; maybe she learns he is adopted, just as she is; perhaps she hears him sing at a company party and recognizes that they both have a passion for vintage Beatles music.

All of a sudden, she is gifted with several categories—several kinship groups—that they in fact share. Were she to shift her thoughts about him from an emphasis on Latino and a man (different) to gourmet cook and a Beatles fan who can sing "Hey Jude" (the same), she has created a new kinship group of which they both are members. He is no longer a "them"; he is now an "us." It is at that point that the healing of even the most subconscious of biases can begin.

I am glad to report that this shifting of kinship groups is one of the easiest things the rational mind can do. As Dr. Kurzban taught us in Chapter 1, we may be compelled to categorize, but just what those categories are is largely up to us.

This is very good news for the cause of bias reduction because, when we shift people from "them" to "us," a couple of positive changes immediately occur.

The first change is based on the fact that human beings tend to see members of other groups as all alike; in essence, we indulge in inflexible generalities (biases) about "them" just because they are not "us." On the other hand, we see members of our own group as individuals who are different from each other in a variety of ways. So, once we are an "us," we automatically see our fellow kinship group members with a less biased eye.

The second thing that this conversion from "them" to "us" accomplishes also has to do with how we perceive people. When we think of others as different from ourselves—as members of another kinship group—we tend to amplify the characteristic that makes them different (skin color, disability, gender, age, etc.). Because that difference is amplified, we notice it first. In turn, because we notice it first, we use that difference as a rubric by which we classify the entire group.

This process gets reversed, however, once we begin to identify that "different" person as one of us. At that point, we focus on what we share and the initial rubric of classification (the thing that made him different) gradually shrinks back to its proper proportion. That difference becomes, at that point, merely one of many characteristics by which we distinguish our new fellow kinship group member.

STRATEGY I: KEEP WHAT WE SHARE TOP-OF-MIND

Do you remember the last time you were in the market for a new car? It is, I know, a long and tedious process consisting of several steps. First, of course, you must decide on your budget. Next, you undertake that sometimes difficult task of deciding just what brand and model you want.

One requirement you might have for a car is that it be fairly unusual; one that you don't often see on the road. The snag in this criterion is that you may not see many of them before you decide on the model, but, much to your dismay, once you make the decision, they, like magic, appear to be everywhere!

"Where did all those cars suddenly come from?" you wonder. In fact, it's not the number of automobiles that has changed, but rather your awareness of that particular model. Once you decided you wanted it, the car became forefront, or top-of-mind, in your thinking. Now top-of-mind, your chosen model no longer blended in with every other vehicle on the freeway and you noticed it everywhere. These heightened observation skills happen because of a fundamental truth of how the mind works:

We notice what we care about.

Though this tendency to notice what we care about may result in disappointment when it comes to buying the only car of a chosen model on the block, the principle of top-of-mind thinking sure comes in handy as we struggle to identify what we share with others.

Keeping what we share top-of-mind is a matter of caring. Once we recognize how important identifying commonalities is to bias reduction, we will care. And, in turn, we will—like in the example of that coveted new car—see shared values, interests, and points of view in every corner of our workplace.

Reader Exploration Point: Over the next two weeks, make an effort to notice 10 interests or life experiences that you share with colleagues whom you used to think were largely different from yourself. You may learn these through conversation or maybe just through observation. As you discover them, write them down. You might be surprised at what you find.

STRATEGY II: PRACTICE SKILLS FOR ACHIEVING EMPATHY

Theatrical coach Konstantin Stanislavsky may not have realized it when he developed an acting technique called the "Magic If," but he was providing us with a strategy for forming common kinship groups and, thereby, reducing bias. Stanislavsky knew that the odds that an actor, even one as dedicated as Marlon Brando, would have actually lived the life of his character (Brando, for all his colorful personality, never was the head of an Italian crime family) are so remote that the only way for him to engage with the part is to ask himself this question: How would I act *if* I had this character's life experience?

There is only one way that the actor can answer that question— identify experiences of his own that approximate those of the character. In short, the Magic If allows one human being to engage emotionally with the experience of another. The Magic If is empathy. There are many definitions of the word *empathy,* but this is the one that serves our purposes best.

The capacity for participating in or relating to another person's feelings.

In connection with our current task of identifying what we share, the empathy we are seeking is summarized in this question: What emotions or experiences—positive or negative—have you had that are, to some degree, like those experienced by someone who otherwise seems different from you? Those shared experiences and emotions, that empathy, becomes, in essence, a shared kinship group.

For those of you who question the possibility of achieving empathy between kinship groups who possess substantially different amounts of power and who have been subjected to substantially different intensities of bias, I sympathize with your skepticism. Full understanding of another's life experience is elusive if, as my father used to say, you haven't "been there." Even if you *have* been there, it is you that was there, not the other person. Everyone's psychological terrain is different. Because of this, the fallout from a given experience will settle on each of us in a unique pattern—deeper here, just a dusting over there. For one person, the fallout may not stick at all; for someone else, it may pile so deep that it suffocates any chance of happiness.

In light of these differences, it is lucky that the following statement is true:

Full understanding is not a prerequisite to empathy.

What we are after—and what we can realistically expect—is a reasonably well-considered grasp of the essence of what the other person has felt or is feeling.

Take labor pains, for example. "You'd have to experience it to understand" is what my mother used to say about giving birth. It was as if one needed to be a member of an exclusive club to comprehend that particularly eloquent "discomfort" (as they called it in natural childbirth classes— ha!). I agree with my mother on this one: If you've never had a baby, you'll never know the full depth of the "discomfort." At the same time, it is still possible to "get it" enough to meet the needs of a woman in labor and to have an intelligent conversation about what she is experiencing.

To notch the pain down a peg or two (and broaden the metaphor to both genders), let's talk about headaches. Everybody's head hurts at one time or another. Some endure the steady drone of a tension headache, while others feel a burning sensation in their sinuses; for the most severely afflicted, their curse is the blinding agony of a migraine. Having been blessed by the gods, I have never had a migraine headache; I have, however, had my share of tension. Because I haven't "been there" with the pain of dilating capillaries, I am incapable of fully grasping my assistant's suffering when a demon migraine comes to call. I have, however, tasted her discomfort through my tension headaches. So, with a little imagination, I can transport myself into a "virtual being there" and achieve what philosopher George Harris calls a state of sympathetic emotional engagement.[1]

Likewise, the able-bodied woman who is temporarily disabled by a broken leg will never feel the same amount of frustration experienced by a man permanently confined to a wheelchair. She can, however, approximate his emotion and thus feel enough empathy to form, with this man and with others like him, a new kinship group. This particular group would be composed of people who understand, to varying degrees, what it feels like to be limited by a disability.

Like headaches, other pains and pleasures of life fall on a continuum, from slight to intense. It doesn't matter where on that continuum the emotion we have felt falls. What matters is that we have experienced that same feeling to some recognizable degree.

Instructions for practicing the Magic If are simple: As you interact with people who seem different from yourself, look for opportunities to identify positive or negative emotions and experiences that you share. Again, the emotions do not have to be of equal intensity to qualify as a match. In Appendix B of this book, you will find several vignettes that you can use to practice the Magic If strategy. As you read them over, and as you encounter people in the workplace, I encourage you to watch for a spark of recognition, a moment of familiarity, or a pang of memory from a time when you felt a similar emotion or found yourself in a similar position.

Here are examples of people who have practiced the Magic If. This practice allowed them to empathize and build a common kinship group with someone whom they previously thought was completely different from themselves.

1. Carol is angry and frustrated when someone falsely accuses her of homophobia. Because of those emotions, she is able to approximate the pain of, and empathize with the frustration of, a male colleague falsely accused of sexism.

2. A Christian is hurt when he overhears a colleague make a negative remark about his religion. Because of that emotion, he is able to empathize with a Muslim colleague who is constantly faced with negative media reports about her spiritual beliefs. Next time he sees the woman, he stops to engage her in conversation.

3. Camilla decides to change jobs because her boss won't give her assignments that are challenging enough to utilize all her skills. When confronted, the boss defends himself by saying he was concerned that the extra stress would aggravate Camilla's multiple sclerosis (Guerilla Bias). Because of this experience, Camilla is able to empathize with an Asian colleague whose manager failed to give her honest feedback out of fear of causing her to lose face.

4. A white male engineer goes to work for a Chinese-owned company and finds he has difficulty fitting in with the culture. Because of this, he begins to empathize with the parents of the immigrant children at his daughter's school who sometimes also feel out of place. At the next school open house, he approaches the family and tries to make them feel welcome.

5. Lourdes always finds it easier to speak her native Spanish when around other Latinas in the workplace. She never understood why her English-speaking colleagues were so uncomfortable with her doing this and assumed they were just biased against immigrants. Then, one day, she found herself in the cafeteria surrounded by people speaking only Vietnamese. This made her feel excluded and ill at ease. Ever since then she has understood how other people feel when she talks Spanish in their presence.

STRATEGY III: SEEK CONTACT WITH THOSE WHO ARE DIFFERENT FROM YOU

Of all the strategies for identifying shared kinship groups, this one seems to be the most straightforward: Spend time with and get to know people who are different from you. On the surface, this is simple. It might mean sitting next to someone different in the cafeteria, stopping in the hall to have a conversation with a teammate whom you barely know, or joining a club whose members are from many different kinship groups .

Theoretically, all this is great. But what happens if that contact is tainted by the lens of the very bias you are trying to beat? That would, of course, defeat the purpose. You could be with the object of your bias for years and still get nowhere if your perception of what he is like continues to conform to your stereotype. How can you identify what you share and, in turn, form a bias-reducing kinship group if you can't see your new acquaintance accurately? The answer is, you can't. What you can do, however, is employ our old friend, the rational brain, to minimize that inaccuracy.

Understand the Process of Distortion

As we saw earlier in this book, being aware of our biases and how they function has an almost magical ability to clear things up. That magic is again at work here. If we can understand how and why our biases are distorting what we see, we are much more likely to control that distortion.

Think of your bias as similar to a pair of rose-tinted glasses through which you are watching a landscape. Because you are aware that the glasses are in the way and have a rough idea of how they function to change the color of what you see, you are not deluded into thinking that the trees and grass have a pinkish cast. The same applies to biases; the more aware you are of the mischief they cause and how the process works, the better your vision will be.

The reason biases are so effective at distorting our view is because of one simple truth: Human beings don't like to be wrong. Have you ever believed something for years when, out of the blue, you were faced with evidence that you had been mistaken all along? Pretty hard to accept, isn't it?

Workplace Application: The 3/2/1 Process

The 3/2/1 Process is intended to facilitate the identification of what we share with people whom we normally might think are very different from ourselves. It consists of the following steps:

Step I: Make contact with three people whom you do not know well and whom you believe to have different values and interests from your own. This contact might be stopping to talk in the hall, approaching them in the gym, or offering to share a cup of coffee during a break.

Step II: Talk to each of those people about two subjects that you might, in the past, have felt would not interest them.

Step III: On the basis of the commonalities you discover, identify one of these people as someone to cultivate further.

When evidence comes our way that we are wrong about something, we are reluctant to change our minds. This is especially true when that "something" is as emotionally charged as a bias. In the case of bias, this reluctance is manifested in a desperate struggle to prove—despite the evidence in front of us—that what we previously believed about the group in question was correct. That's exactly what Linda, the HR director, in Chapter 5, did when she saw that Mariko did not conform to her stereotype of Japanese women (shy, retiring, and not good sales material). Rather than admit that her bias was wrong, Linda aided it in its distortion by rationalizing what she saw in Mariko to fit what she previously believed about the applicant's character and skills. Linda's rationalization, you may recall, consisted of her saying to herself, "Mariko is just pretending to be assertive."

Another way biases distort our view is by manipulating us into seeing what we expect to see. I'll spare you most of the physiological details, but the bottom line is this: If incoming stimuli correspond to our expectations—in this case, our biases—they are reinforced by the brain and conducted onward. If the stimuli do not correspond to our expectations, the brain suppresses the signal. For example, if we expect that our new female boss will fail to give us opportunities (Bias: "All women who succeed then turn their backs on the women that follow"), then we will begin to notice every time she gives a man a plum assignment. By the same token, we will fail to notice the times she helps a women out. To make matters worse, not only do we notice those things that conform to our bias, but we also actually search them out and give them extra weight, while ignoring evidence that our bias is wrong.

Focus Your Thoughts on Individual Characteristics

Beyond remaining vigilant to how biases (like those rose-tinted glasses) distort our view, there is a second way we can use the rational brain to see more clearly: Employ the strategy put forth by Susan Fiske back in Chapter 1. She suggested, you may recall, that when spending time with people toward whom we have a bias, we can minimize the distorting power of that belief by inwardly asking questions about the needs and characteristics of each individual we meet. This question asking has a way of focusing our thoughts on individual characteristics and, thereby, correcting the distortion our bias might otherwise have created.

Managers, I am glad to report, have the ability to positively influence how much of this "individuation"—seeing people as individuals—goes on. Research in the area of bias reduction has proven that, if team members are instructed by an authority figure to focus on individual qualities rather than collective characteristics, they are more apt to do so.[2] That is indeed good news for managers looking for positive steps they can take to reduce bias in their workplaces.

STRATEGY IV: CREATE WORKPLACE OPPORTUNITIES FOR CROSS-GROUP CONTACT

Organizations can play a major role in facilitating bias reduction by creating ways for people of diverse backgrounds to be together and, in turn, have the opportunity to discover and focus on what they share. This

Workplace Application: Tips for Creating and Encouraging Corporate Kinship Groups

Establishing affinity/networking groups along the lines of shared interests is one way to encourage new kinships groups. If your organization, however, is too small for that approach, there are still many other ways you can orchestrate the kind of familiarity that will create a sense of shared community.

1. **Information Sharing through Articles:** Invite representatives of various kinship groups to write brief articles about their values, hobbies, and life experiences. These might be posted on the company Web site or published in its newsletter. Example: A white man writes about the challenges and joys of raising a child with a disability. This, in turn, helps nonwhite team members connect with his love of family rather than just his "whiteness." A blind person might write about her love of gardening, thereby enabling others to see her, and other people with disabilities, as multifaceted human beings.

2. **Social Activities:** Arrange for outside-of-work social activities and orchestrate them so that participants will be encouraged to mix with colleagues whom they do not know.

3. **Hobbies:** Set up lunchtime sessions around shared hobbies and promote them among all segments of the workforce.

4. **Mentor Programs:** Design a two-way mentoring program. General Mills and Chase Bank of Texas, for example, have had great success with this strategy. In this approach, the mentor partners are not only at different levels in the organization, but also of different ethnic, racial, or gender backgrounds. The other key element is that the partners are equally responsible for sharing information about themselves and their cultures. Programs such as these result in two-way learning, increased understanding between diverse groups of people, and enhanced empathy.

5. **Volunteerism:** Orchestrate volunteer efforts that bring team members of diverse backgrounds together around a shared effort and common goal.

6. Individual Presentations: Set aside time at regularly scheduled meetings for team members of different backgrounds to talk briefly about their cultures, interests, or challenges. Encourage others in attendance to ask questions and share similar experiences or feelings. (See also Appendix B for activities that will facilitate this sharing process.)

contact, in order to be most effective at reducing bias, needs to have the following characteristics:

1. Be appropriately intimate
2. Be as varied as possible
3. Be sanctioned by a relevant authority figure
4. Be among people who are reasonably equal in status and resources
5. Should be, if possible, unhurried
6. Be goal oriented

Affinity/network/employee resource groups certainly conform to these requirements and have for years been the backbone of diversity efforts in many companies. Ever since they were first conceived in the late 1970s, affinity groups have been organized around some shared identity. Initially, they focused on shared ethnicity and race. Then they branched out to include women's groups, and, still later, shared sexual orientation. Groups such as these have long served important functions, not only as employee support opportunities, but also as valuable business resources for the organizations of which they are a part.

It is relatively recently, however, that corporations have taken the concept of affinity groups one step further and, thereby, begun to use them, whether they realized it or not, to defeat bias in their workplaces. These newer groups are organized not around difference (women as different than men; Latinos as different from Asians), but around what people, who might be different in ethnicity, race, sexual orientation or gender, have in common. This commonality might be a shared interest, life challenge, or any other unifying factor. No matter what its nature, that shared interest is a kinship group that brings people who are otherwise different together.

Examples of such groups are growing; here are just a few.

- Interfaith Network (Ford Motor Company)
- Veterans Affinity Group (General Motors)
- Military Reservists (Microsoft)
- Part-Time Workers (Abbott Laboratories)
- Parents at Amex (American Express)
- Adoption Network (AstraZeneca)
- Deaf/Hard of Hearing (Microsoft)
- Dads at Microsoft (Microsoft)
- Family Caregivers Network (Kimberly-Clark)
- FlexImpact [for employees working flextime] (Microsoft)
- Junior Exempt Employee Forum (Booz Allen Hamilton)
- Attention Deficit Disorder (Microsoft)

Affinity groups are, however, not the only way organizations can orchestrate the identification of kinship groups. Any kind of club, volunteer program, or social event at which people mix will do the job. Northrop Grumman, for example, has numerous clubs, many of which meet during the noon hour to organize their free-time activities. These clubs are focused on a wide variety of interests including, among others, cigars, cooking, vintage aircraft, scrapbooking, karaoke, and even on the bumpy thrills of four-wheel driving. Amgen, a leader in human therapeutics and biotechnology, is another club-conscious organization. It encourages the formation of kinship groups around interests such as Toastmasters, soccer, and bicycling. Amgen employees even have the opportunity to join the company's very own salsa band. Similarly, medical technology manufacturer Gen-Probe brings employees together around physical activities such as aerobics classes, sand volleyball games, and yoga instruction.

Bank of America bridges the distinction between clubs and volunteer efforts by sending its Bank of America Singers into retirement homes to entertain the residents. It is in this world of volunteerism where some of the most significant kinship groups can be formed. This is because volunteer efforts combine time together with that all-important kinship group–forming element—a common goal.

The Xerox Leadership Association beautifully illustrates this kinship-producing formula. Its membership consists of diverse people who arrange for charitable activities during which Xerox employees of all backgrounds can mix. Another example is Macy's Partners in Time program, which yearly brings together 67,000 employees, families, and friends to volunteer in various programs throughout the country. Key Bank of Oregon is yet another good example. The bank closes its branches once a year at one o'clock in the afternoon, leaving only a skeleton crew in charge. The rest of the team disperses into the community to work in homeless shelters and perform other valuable services such as cleaning gutters for the elderly.

Whether it be through the formation of affinity groups, social clubs, or volunteer efforts, the options for bringing diverse team members together are limited only by your imagination, your resources, and your corporate goals.

STRATEGY V: CREATE AND EMPHASIZE SHARED GOALS

Have you ever been stuck in an elevator? I'll wager that when this happened, you and your fellow prisoners abandoned all pretense of conventional elevator etiquette. You no longer stood erect and stared forward, looking neither to the left nor to the right. And, certainly, you no longer pretended you were alone. Also, once the reality set in that the elevator was malfunctioning, any fine distinctions about who belonged to what demographic category instantly dissolved; you were now all members of a newly created kinship group.

This particular kinship group was composed of people who had in common the stark terror of being trapped in a small space, being out of control, and possessing no knowledge of when or how the adventure would end. The group also had a shared goal: get out of there, and the sooner, the better.

Of course, a kinship group born of a temporary experience like being trapped in an elevator has a short life span; but the principle of sharing a common goal applies equally to more lasting situations. Alice, the one who made such a mess of that receptionist's desk earlier in this chapter, understood this. Alice, by the way, ended up getting a job and eventually recovered from the pain of being treated so badly by that racist executive. Unfortunately, however, the new job wasn't all that much better. They hired Alice, you see, not because they particularly wanted her, but because they were afraid that, if they didn't, they would be sued.

As a result of this attitude, her new white office mates were standoffish at best, and she could still feel racism in the air. Alice, however, wasn't willing to accept working in an atmosphere of dissension. She set out to fix the situation and did so by figuring out a way to bring the group together behind a common project. Although Alice didn't realize it at the time, she was creating a new kinship group.

Her idea was simple. She asked her colleagues if they would work with her to design ways to improve the functioning of the department. Fortunately, they agreed and a new kinship group was born, a group whose members now shared something that had previously been missing: a specific and measurable goal. Although the creation of a shared goal was not enough to instantly dissolve the racism in the hearts of Alice's colleagues, their common effort did provide a medium of familiarity. And familiarity, as we have seen, is an important first step to reducing any type of conscious or unconscious bias.

Shared goals, you see, have the power to fill the fissure that separates us. When we are striving to achieve the same thing, it is just plain harder to hate each other. Roger Ackerman, former CEO of Corning, knows this. Roger grew up in the 1950s and played every sport you could name. His enthusiasm for athletics taught him a fundamental truth that has as much to do with bias as it does with sports.

"When in the heat of battle, it doesn't matter what you are."

Another corporate leader, Jim Adamson, whom we met earlier, had the same experience when first entering an otherwise all black high school. Jim, who is white, had trouble fitting in—until he and his fellow students picked up a basketball and headed for the court. Once he became a really good player, any concern his black teammates had about the color of Jim's skin melted in the heat of their enthusiasm for winning the game.

The unifying power of "winning the game"—no matter the name of that game—applies as much to the corporate world as it does to the basketball court. Once a goal is set and committed to, the differences on the

Other Benefits to Identifying Shared Kinship Groups

1. A kinship group places the emphasis on similarity rather than difference. The more similar to us we think a person is, the more empathy we feel toward them. This empathy, in turn, creates a more productive working relationship.

2. The recognition of shared values and goals on a team produces increased personal satisfaction and enhanced commitment to the task.

3. Diverse teams in which the members are socially connected—as in a kinship group—outperform teams of relative strangers when bits of information held by the various individuals are necessary for the success of the project.

4. Diverse team members who have identified commonalities feel more secure and, in turn, are more comfortable sharing their unique ideas and information.

5. Once we see a person as a member of our kinship group, we tend to have broader experiences with her and, in turn, are able to see her individual qualities more readily.

team become secondary to the effort to meet that goal. The goal creates a kinship group.

MGM Mirage provides us with an example of a common goal, and, therefore, shared kinship group, that some of you might have duplicated without even realizing it. Like many of your organizations, MGM Mirage has chosen to drive its diversity and bias-reduction efforts through the recruitment and training of Diversity Champions. At this writing, it has approximately 6,000 Diversity Champions who are trained in diversity issues and deployed as "agents of change" throughout the culture.

For our purposes, a key element of the MGM Mirage approach to diversity is that it encourages the involvement of people of all backgrounds. Many white males, for example, have enthusiastically signed on as Champions. This points up the fact that the program serves a double function. The first function is, of course, to spread the message of inclusion throughout the organization. The second is to create a shared goal toward which team members of diverse backgrounds can strive. As such, MGM Mirage's Diversity Champion program is a bias-reducing kinship group.

CONCLUSION: IDENTIFY A SHARED HUMANITY

In recent years, I have undertaken a task that has taught me more about the humanity we share than any other experience of my life. I have begun raising puppies for an organization called Canine Companions for Independence; one of these dogs, a yellow retriever named Rye, is warming my toes as I type these words. The idea is that we raise and train the puppy, give it back for six months of professional training, and then, if all goes well, eventually have the honor of seeing it placed as an assistance dog to a person with a disability.

This process of raising a puppy is obviously filled with rich emotional experiences, many of which result from encounters with the wide variety of people that the dog attracts. For example, as I walk into a restaurant or through a mall or into a movie theater with a puppy named Mikki—a yellow Labrador–golden retriever mix festooned in her blue and yellow CCI cape—people of all descriptions approach me to ask about the dog or to beg the favor of a short session of ear scratching (the dog's, not the person's).

It is because of these puppies that I have had lengthy conversations with college professors, immigrants, and homeless people, all of whom are drawn to either the love of dogs or the notion of helping someone with a disability. Whether we talk because of the dog or the disability, it is the human connection that counts. That human connection—that humanity—is, come to think about it, the ultimate kinship group.

CHAPTER SUMMARY

- One way to diminish both conscious and unconscious bias is to broaden and multiply the number of kinship groups to which we belong. When we form a shared kinship group with an object of our bias, he is automatically transformed from the status of "them" to "us." This transformation allows us to see the person as an individual—not as a member of a group—and to focus more on what we share.

- The more we care about what we share, the more we will keep that sharing top-of-mind. Therefore, the more we will notice commonalities with other groups.

- A key strategy for identifying common kinship groups is for us to empathize with the emotions and experiences of those who are otherwise very different from ourselves. This common feeling, even if it is to a different degree, automatically creates a connection and constitutes a kinship group that reduces our biases.

- Making contact with people who are different from ourselves can give rise to new kinship groups by providing the opportunity to identify what we share.

- Affinity/networking groups formed around shared interests, along with clubs and volunteer efforts, automatically create new kinship groups. Any activity that brings diverse people together in new combinations serves as an effective bias-reduction strategy.

- Common goals are essentially a form of kinship group.

STEP SIX: SHOVE YOUR BIASES ASIDE

CHAPTER FOCUS QUESTION

How can I move my biases out of the way so they no longer block and distort my view?

Some years ago, I was strolling down a street in Los Angeles—nice part of town, broad daylight, lots of people around. I was also, and this is an important detail, a perfectly safe distance from the curb. As I walked, a car pulled up beside me, slowed down, and stopped. Just as I turned to look at the car, the driver lowered his head so I could see his face. The moment I saw his skin was black, I jumped back. I then had one of those uncomfortable moments that make life so interesting, when the driver said, with great dignity and compassion, "That's OK; I understand." He then asked for directions and continued on his way.

Because this incident took place many years ago, long before I began my own journey through the Vision Renewal Process, I'll give myself a break for reacting so defensively. The question still remains, however, "Would I jump again today?" The truth? I honestly don't know. My guess is I would have the urge to jump. But I trust that my mindfulness of my bias, "All black men are potentially dangerous in some way," would empower me to shove the bias aside, at least long enough to see the driver for who he most likely would be: a man whose GPS is on the blink.

It is this shoving aside of our biases that the first five Vision Renewal Process steps were designed to make possible.

- Steps One and Two made us aware of what we were fighting and showed us where to focus our energies.
- Step Three ("Identify the Secondary Gains of Your Biases") helped us realize that any benefit we think we get from a bias is not worth the price we pay.
- Step Four ("Dissect Your Biases") showed us the weak foundation on which our biases are built and, thereby, helped us think more rationally.
- Step Five ("Identify Common Kinship Groups") helped us shift our focus from how we differ to what we share.

Now, it's time to reap the benefit of all this hard work. Essentially, what these first steps did was transform each target bias from a vital force with the power to distort our perceptions, into an inert object that can be picked up and moved anytime it gets in our way. Our biases have, in short, been objectified and converted into nothing more threatening than an irritating habit of thought.

You may have noticed that this is a short chapter. That is because there isn't much to say about Step Six.

Think the thought, shove it aside; think the thought, shove it aside; think the thought, shove it aside.

Simple.

As we have seen, bias is an attitude, and every attitude at some point is manifested as a thought. So far, we're OK—what we think, although not always good for us, is usually harmless. That is, unless we allow that thought to dictate a behavior. It is between the biased thought and the action that we want to throw the switch.

Because Jill was such a hard case, I'm going to use her as an example. Jill had what seemed to be an unshakable bias against people over 50. Here's how that bias/thought/behavior progression played out in her case:

- *Jill's Underlying Bias:* All people over 50 are uncreative and stuck in the past.
- *Jill's Thought:* "There is no point in giving Lance that assignment; he'll never come up with the innovation we need."
- *Jill's Behavior:* She refuses to give Lance any challenging projects.
- *Consequence:* Lance quits the organization because of lack of opportunity and takes his 25 years of experience elsewhere.

Remember, Jill has already gone through the first five steps, so now she has the power to stop this train wreck and keep Lance from leaving. The point where Jill needs to switch tracks is just after the thought, "There is no point in giving Lance that assignment" comes into her head. The trick to doing this, for Jill and for us, is to stay in the moment so we can catch the thought as it whizzes by. This takes practice and vigilance, but it can be done. Also, it helps to realize an important principle.

Shoving a thought out of your mind is a mechanical act.

We are not our thoughts. Our thoughts are tools that we produce to help us survive. Because we produce them, we can manipulate them. In short, we have the power to follow these instructions.

Think the thought, shove it aside; think the thought, shove it aside; think the thought, shove it aside.

Even if we only keep the biased thought out of the way for a few seconds, we can peer through that break in the fog and see the person more accurately. Perhaps the fog will close again, but it is a start and, like any mechanical act, shoving the thought aside becomes easier with practice.

The benefits, however, of shoving a bias aside go far beyond the ability to see one individual clearly. For one thing, the more we do it, the easier it gets; eventually, manipulating our biases becomes a habit of which we are barely aware.

Another benefit lies in the fact that bias-free vision has a cumulative effect. Because it allows us to see people clearly, we suddenly find ourselves meeting more and more individuals who do not conform to our bias. At first, this reality tempts us to think that "they" have changed, evolved, and, in some ways, gotten better. In fact, it is *we* who have evolved; it is we who have, in many ways, gotten better.

As experiences of seeing people accurately accumulate, the balance between past biases and real life begins to tip in favor of accuracy, and the biases begin to fade. Ultimately, cases of mistaken identity become rare occurrences that surprise us rather than daily events of which we are not-so-blissfully unaware.

CHAPTER SUMMARY

- Once we have laid the proper foundation, shoving our biases aside becomes a mechanical act of habit and will.
- The more we practice pushing our biases out of the way, the easier it becomes until, eventually, we do it automatically.
- Seeing people clearly has a cumulative effect. The more we are able to see people as individuals, without the intervening distortion of our bias, the more evidence we will have that our bias is wrong.

CHAPTER

10

STEP SEVEN: FAKE IT TILL YOU MAKE IT

CHAPTER FOCUS QUESTION

What do I do if I just can't seem to get rid of my bias?

Sally was sure it had gone—her long-held bias that perpetually whispered in her ear, "All women are better at building relationships than men are." But, there it was again. Just as she was about to interview a woman for a newly opened supervisory position, up that pesky bias popped, making its unwanted appearance in the form of this thought: "I'm sure, because she's a woman, this candidate will be a better team builder than the men I'm interviewing later this afternoon."

Sally's example forces us to face the sad reality that some biases simply refuse to stay out of our way. For whatever reason, every time we are convinced that our inflexible belief is finally and forever jettisoned from our brains, it comes meandering back like an unwanted houseguest. Fortunately for us all, this return is not the end of the story—there is still more we can do, not only to keep the bias from doing damage, but also to finalize its extinction.

FAKE YOUR BEHAVIORS

In the event that you find your mind occupied by a seemingly inde-structible bias, remember that there is still hope. That hope lies in a simple suggestion:

Act as if you don't have the bias.

Aristotle was a fan of this approach. He knew that attitude follows behavior. With respect to bias he would no doubt have supported the modern dictum, "Fake it till you make it."

Psychologist Daryl Bem put it another way: "Saying and doing becomes believing."[1] The psychological truism that underpins this statement is that most of us can't stand doing something that does not conform to what we really believe. This disconnect between action and belief is called "cognitive dissonance" and it comes into play with both conscious and unconscious biases. Because cognitive dissonance is so unpleasant, something has to give, and if we are stuck with the behavior, we are forced by our discomfort to change our attitude.

The impact of cognitive dissonance is supported by a good deal of research, including one Yale study in which students were paid various amounts of money to write essays taking a position they did not hold. Those who were paid the least ended up changing their view to conform to what they wrote in the essay; those who were paid the most continued to sustain a position that was different from what they had written.

Why do you think the poorly paid students changed their attitudes, while the better-compensated ones stuck to their original opinion? The answer is that the extra money allowed the better-paid students to more easily justify their deception. They had, after all, been given a substantial amount to act in a way that was dissonant with their beliefs—that is, to write an essay with which they did not agree. A reasonable person, the students concluded, would betray their values for this much compensation.

The money, in essence, bought them out of the discomfort caused by the inconsistency between belief and action. The poorly paid students lacked the luxury of this excuse. The only way they could continue to feel like honest people was to change their attitude and, thereby, undo the deception. With respect to bias, if we act as if we are not biased toward a kinship group—act in a way different from our attitude—the discomfort caused by the incongruity might just force us to change how we feel.

I have created a composite character named Bess to show how beneficial faking behavior can be. Ever since she can remember, Bess has had, as she put it, a "thing" about people who don't express themselves well in English. Whether the reason is that English is their second language or that they lack formal education, as soon as she hears them speak, her mind is filled with judgments like "unintelligent," "will never be able to do the job" (even if the job has little to do with communication skills), "uncreative," and "doesn't have much to contribute." Bess had the luxury of being aware of her bias so was able to enter into the systematic behavior change I am about to describe. Even if she hadn't, however, even if the belief were subconscious, the very fact that she went through the motions of treating people more fairly would inevitably register in her brain and, if continued long enough, almost certainly weaken her bias.

For whatever reason, Bess just couldn't exterminate this bias. She was aware it existed and aware it distorted her view of many employees who had much to offer the organization. However, she still found herself avoiding people who did not articulate up to her standard. The problem became so bad that one staff member, a Latino immigrant, went to Bess and said he felt she was discriminating against him. Fortunately, they were able to work together to avoid any legal action. But the incident was, for a while, very disruptive to the diverse work team that Bess's manager was trying so hard to develop.

Fictional Bess felt awful about this incident. Determined to change her behavior, she made a list of the things her bias was causing her to do and the consequences of those behaviors:

1. *Behavior:* Failure to initiate conversations with certain employees. *Negative consequences:* Perception of discrimination. Alienation of the team.
2. *Behavior:* Failure to assign select team members to plum projects. *Negative consequences:* Employees' inability to gain valuable experience and exposure. Perception (or reality) of discrimination.

3. *Behavior:* Failure to call on particular employees during meetings. *Negative consequences:* Employees' missed opportunities to voice ideas or ask questions. Unheard ideas that might have benefited the organization. Perception (or reality) of discrimination.

Having made her behaviors and their consequences concrete and measurable, Bess set out to do things differently:

1. *Substitute behavior:* Bess consciously began to initiate conversations with people whom she used to ignore.
   Positive Consequences: She discovered how much they had to offer, began to feel better about them, and, in turn, started treating them more fairly.
2. *Substitute behavior:* Bess began deliberately assigning those employees who were qualified to good projects. Notice, I said, "those who were qualified"; she resisted the temptation to substitute her own bias for a Guerilla Bias.
   Positive Consequence: Most of the employees excelled.
3. *Substitute behavior:* Bess began to call on people more equally during meetings and, most important, really listen to what they had to say.
   Positive Consequences: She and her team were exposed to different perspectives. Also, the employees were able to gradually hone their communication skills.

The ultimate consequence of these changes in behavior was that Bess's bias began to fade. It faded for two reasons. First, it faded because the dissonance (the difference) between her behavior and her biased attitude subconsciously bothered Bess. The two could not cohabit in the same person. Fortunately, in Bess's case, it was the bias that moved out first.

The second reason her bias faded was that it just couldn't survive the onslaught of positive and varied information that Bess's new behaviors caused to come her way. The better she treated people, the better they responded; the better they responded, the more positive her experience; the more positive her experience, the better she felt about a group whom she had previously dismissed. In Bess's case, each positive experience served as a layer of poultice on her festering bias. Before she knew it, the wound had healed. Fake it till you make it; it works.

FAKE YOUR LANGUAGE

I know, this "fake your language" idea sounds weird and even a bit unethical. You'll feel better knowing that I am not suggesting you lie, nor am I asking you to parrot phrases out of a dictionary of political correctness. I am asking you to do something you do most of the time anyway: Use respectful language. The "faking" comes in on those occasions when you are not feeling particularly respectful.

One of the benefits of speaking respectfully is obvious. Speaking respectfully to and about people produces, of course, the same positive responses that Bess experienced when she changed her behaviors. Those responses will, as they did in Bess's case, provide the kind of positive feedback that can't help but erode bias. Speaking respectfully, however, has another, more mysterious, bias-reducing quality.

What we say can become what we believe.

This idea comes from the work of anthropologist Jennifer James, and I think she's onto something. Dr. James contends that if we say something out loud enough times, we will eventually come to believe it.[2] If this is true, and I believe it is, then speaking negatively of a kinship group, telling inappropriate jokes, and using disrespectful language cannot be a good thing.

On the other hand, if we curb negative language and instead speak positively and respectfully of others, those positive words might just begin to seep into our minds and change how we feel. What this amounts to is adopting a personally correct (not politically correct) lexicon that not only is more pleasant for others, but also helps us move slowly, but surely, toward a more enlightened attitude.

FAKE YOUR THOUGHTS

Along the same lines, there is evidence that faking thoughts, just like faking behaviors and language, can change attitudes. The *Harvard Business Review* reports that even imagining or fantasizing about groups being a certain way can, at the very least temporarily, reduce bias.[3]

Workplace Application: Install Safeguards against Bias-tainted Decisions

Both organizations and individuals pay a steep price for decisions that are driven by bias rather than reality. In no arena is this truer than in the area of hiring and promotions. For this reason, it is wise to install safeguards as a protection against bias-tainted decisions.

1. Describe job requirements in as much detail, and as concretely, as possible. The more precise the description, the less apt a subjective bias is to squeeze its way in and distort the decision-making process.

2. Construct panels of interviewers who are of diverse backgrounds and points of view. The actual makeup of this group will depend on whom is being interviewed and what the various attitudes of the interviewing team might be. Keep in mind that the variety of backgrounds you pick may have nothing to do with visible diversity; it could involve diversity of attitude and life experience instead. Also, the interviewers may or may not need to be of the same background as the candidate.

3. Before beginning the interview, make mental or physical notes of what you expect the candidate to be like according to her name, picture, or any other information available. Next, examine these expectations in light of the strategies in this book to assess if they might reflect a bias. Finally, if you suspect bias, do everything you can to keep these thoughts from distorting your perception of the candidate.

4. If you are interviewing for an in-house promotion, rely on a 360-degree feedback strategy to increase the chances of getting a clear picture of what the candidate has to offer.

5. Take a few minutes during the interview to ask questions that have nothing to do with the job. Within the boundaries, of course, of the law, inquire about hobbies and other outside interests. Include additional questions that will force you to see the candidate as an individual, not just as a member of a group. This strategy of focusing on the individual is a powerful tool for reducing the impact of bias.

6. Similarly, take time to identify things you, the interviewer, have in common with the candidate. Not only will this identification of shared kinship groups help to diffuse any bias you may have, but the process will also make the candidate more comfortable—and, therefore, more likely to interview well.

7. If you feel you have an inflexible belief that will prevent you from making a fair decision, step aside. There is no shame in this, and it is far better than allowing a bias to result in an unwise, or even discriminatory, decision.

That certainly is an intriguing idea, but I'm not suggesting you sit around fantasizing about the objects of your bias. I have something more practical in mind. My idea is more along the lines of *faking out* your thoughts and, thereby, manipulating them into being what you want them to be. This isn't the first time we have touched on the idea of manipulating our thoughts. That's essentially what Susan Fiske is saying when she encourages us to inwardly ask questions about individual characteristics. The strategy proposed here is another take on that theme.

Let's look, for example, at how we might trick our brains into making better decisions about whom to promote. I can explain this best by first examining how this task is normally handled. In most cases, the first step is to construct a list of those qualified candidates who readily come to mind. Can you see the problem with this approach? If we have a conscious or unconscious bias, be it for or against certain groups, this list of those who "readily come to mind" will certainly reflect that bias.

A better approach—and one that will trick your biased mind into cooperating—is to make a more complete list of candidates. This list would include not merely those who come to mind but every single person who is qualified. Of course, this process will take longer, require you to be more systematic, and no doubt necessitate some research. It is, however, worth the effort.

Constructing such a list serves two purposes. Most obviously, it protects against any bias-generated "amnesia" that might allow you to forget someone whom you should have considered. The second purpose is less obvious.

The very act of considering a counter-bias choice at the conscious level can reduce unconscious bias.

Isn't that amazing? By forcing our brains to consider other options, we are channeling them into unbiased territory. The more we do this, whether it be by asking specific questions about a group as discussed earlier or by considering broader options, the deeper that unbiased channel becomes and the easier it is to access the next time there are decisions to be made.

CHAPTER SUMMARY

- Faking behaviors, language, and thoughts can reduce both conscious and unconscious biases.
- By behaving as if our biased attitude does not exist, not only do we encourage a more positive reaction from the objects of that bias, but the attitude itself is also apt to change to conform to our behavior.
- The words we say can eventually influence what we believe. Therefore, speaking respectfully about and to people can result in attitudes that are more respectful and less biased.
- It is possible to reduce biases by manipulating our thoughts. Imagining people in a positive light and forcing our brains to consider a broader range of candidates for particular positions are two such strategies that can result in changed attitudes.

PART THREE

GATEWAY EVENTS™: ENTERING INTO DIVERSITY DIALOGUE

INTRODUCTION TO PART THREE

GATEWAY EVENTS™: ENTERING INTO DIVERSITY DIALOGUE

No one would say it was a pleasant conversation and no one would dare claim that it didn't take courage to make it happen. It was the mid-1960s and Tony was the only black student at the college. A whiz in chemistry, he sat in class week after week—alone. Six empty seats surrounded him in all directions. That is, until the day Dennis came and sat down beside him, stuck out his hand, and said hello. Dennis, a white student, was tired of submitting to peer pressure that dictated he avoid Tony.

Dennis and Tony began to talk, and Dennis asked some awkward questions. "Why do you want to be with whites anyway? After all, we don't exactly make you feel welcome." "Why aren't most black people very smart?" "Why?" "Why?" "Why?" If there had been a politically correct dictatorship back then, Dennis would have been in trouble—but there wasn't. Dennis took a chance, and Dennis got lucky. Tony had the courage to listen and the wisdom to respond. (Tony, by the way, went on to become diversity director for the American Red Cross.)

Tony and Dennis were willing to risk loss of face, anger, and even humiliation to have a conversation. Also, they were unwilling to tolerate what Bruce Jacobs, in his book *Race Manners,* calls "sterile, exaggerated, civility."[1] You know the kind of thing I mean. It is the kind of civility that a middle-aged black man described to me as the climate of his all-white-but-him neighborhood in Virginia: nice people, no cross burning, and no name-calling—but little else going on, either. Most certainly, no progress being made toward the relief of bias. Jacobs argues that, if we are to make that progress, we need to begin to talk. In the following passage, Jacobs speaks of racial differences, but his words apply just as eloquently to any type of diversity and any type of bias.

From what I have seen of racial card-folding among folks who ought to be arguing, the most dangerous racial assumption is that a black or white acquaintance "won't be able to handle" disagreement or challenge. Please. While zealots are out bombing buildings and burning churches, the rest of us are afraid to talk because we might upset one another? I say let's talk while we can.[2]

Dennis and Tony were willing to talk while they could. They are brave men and Part Three of this book argues that we must follow in their footsteps. We must begin carrying on conversations about bias, because conversation is our most powerful weapon against the fear and misunderstanding that surround us. It is also the most powerful tool we have for fighting bias. It is time we risk hurt feelings, discomfort, and even anger. Like that black man in the "civil" white neighborhood said to me, "At some point, we have to trust that we have something reasonable to say and take a risk." There is a crisis in courage when it comes to bias and we need to wake up to the fact that diversity is a contact sport. Psychic bruises and a bump or two are always possible, but there is virtue in that conflict if it moves us closer to the goal of clearing our vision and seeing people for who they are.

Fortunately, or unfortunately, depending on how you look at it, we rarely have to seek out opportunities to engage in conversations about bias; life has a way of presenting them to us. These opportunities come in the form of misunderstandings, accusations, and any other happenings that involve discord between or about people who are different from each other. Because these incidents are capable of bringing about productive dialogue and thereby serve as gateways to greater understanding and reduced bias, I call them Gateway Events™. Gateway Events appear in many guises. Here are just a few examples:

- Perhaps you witness an inappropriate act or hear a joke or comment that is disrespectful.
- Maybe someone falsely accuses you of bias.
- Perhaps someone treats you in a way that appears to reflect a biased attitude.
- Perhaps you say or do something that inadvertently offends someone.
- Maybe you witness someone else being falsely accused of bias.

- Perhaps you are confused and uncomfortable because of the differences between yourself and someone else.
- Perhaps you say or do something involving diversity that you immediately regret.

Regardless of the nature of the Gateway Event, talking about sticky diversity issues is not always comfortable, and not every conversation ends with the participants collapsing into each other's arms in a mutual paroxysm of newfound understanding. The purpose of Part Three is to provide the tools and skills to minimize the discomfort and maximize the chance that we will, if not collapse into each other's arms, at least be able to walk through those gateways and meet on the other side. Believe me, it is worth the effort.

BENEFIT: INCREASED KNOWLEDGE AND UNDERSTANDING

Here are stories of two very different women. One was willing to take a risk in order to diffuse a bias and thus succeeded in moving the cause of diversity forward. The other allowed her fear of confrontation to seduce her into passing up an opportunity for understanding that would probably never come again.

The woman who was willing to walk bravely through her own personal Gateway Event was Deborah, a restaurateur in San Diego, California. This is what she had to say.

Some years ago, I had an unfortunate relationship with a food-and-beverage manager to whom I reported. After I had been on the job for only a few weeks, he upped my hours, increased my workload, and began to make comments under his breath like, "Female executive chef—what a joke!" To make matters worse, he was uncomfortable with the fact that I was gay. He even told a coworker that he was determined to "drive out the female chef." I tried to talk to him, to get a good relationship going, but he just wouldn't listen. The final blow came during a management meeting, when he and I had a heated difference of opinion. At one point, he was holding a belt that someone had borrowed and returned to him. He slapped his hand with it several times, and said, in front of everyone, that after the meeting he would "teach me a lesson."

As it turns out, I ended up quitting. During my final weeks on the job, I deliberately asked him to attend a local restaurant function with me. During this event, we actually were able to have a civilized conversation about what had happened between us. After this, he tried everything to get me to stay, even apologizing for his behavior and explaining that, in his country, women were third-class citizens and that homosexuals were still publicly stoned. Though it was too little, too late for me, I found it encouraging that he hired another woman to replace me, and he seems to have worked out some of his problems.

Had Deborah not tried to educate this man, he might never have seen the error of his ways. Not only did her successor benefit from Deborah's courage, but so did the entire San Diego restaurant community.

The other woman, the one who backed away from her gateway, was yours truly:

> The scene of my cowardice was the dining room of a Los Angeles restaurant, where I sat facing a young Harvard graduate. This was no ordinary Ivy League scholar but a young Latino who had managed, through sheer grit and intelligence, to pull himself out of the ganglands of East Los Angeles. This book was the catalyst for the lunch, and my intent was to learn as much as possible about what promised to be a unique perspective on diversity and bias. As it turned out, I learned more about myself than I did about him.
>
> For one thing, I began stereotyping this fellow before I'd even laid eyes on him. As I drove to lunch, my head was filled with images—and biases—of a brave young man of superior intelligence, clear thought, and emotional maturity, worthy of every drop of my admiration. After all, I "reasoned," he must be superior in many ways to have achieved so much.
>
> Once the meal and the conversation began, however, it did not take long for my admiration to fade. His anger and his biases, rooted, of course, in the fear- and hate-filled neighborhood of his youth, were so overwhelming that they distorted his view of everything. He may have been bright, but personally and spiritually evolved he was not.

As he spewed invective after invective about how "all" the professors at Harvard were racist and how the content of the courses was little more than conservative propaganda, I just sat there in ill-disguised disillusionment as my Cobb salad wilted and my once-icy lemonade crept toward room temperature. Of course, I might not have been able to help my companion face his biases, but it sure would have been nice had I at least attempted, as Deborah did in her situation, to engage him in conversation about why he felt as he did.

Here was a chance for me to dialogue on these issues, to show that I was willing to disagree with him and risk being accused of bias and white arrogance. Who knows, maybe if I had been honest, if I had been less patronizing, less a practitioner of Guerilla Bias, I would have been able to dampen his anger. Perhaps I could have shown him that not all whites are racist, that not every misspoken word is intended as an attack on his heritage, and that this new world he had worked so hard to enter is not as hostile as he thought.

BENEFIT: THE STIFLED SPREAD OF BIAS

One of the scariest things about bias is that it is contagious. A perfect upbringing might be able to inoculate against the infection, but, unfortunately, that strain of vaccine is in perilously short supply. Once we are infected, either through our parents or by experience, each of us becomes a carrier of the bias bug. This contagion can spread in any environment, but it happens most readily in cultures that are cordial hosts for the disease.

Because of the shortfall of perfect upbringings, we need to face up to some facts.

The responsibility for stifling the spread of bias rests on each of us, and our main method for achieving this goal is conversation.

There are many ways to talk about how this works, but you can't beat good old Ivan Pavlov and those dogs for giving us a clear explanation.

You may remember from high school that this Russian physiologist's goal was to condition his dogs to salivate even in the absence of anything to salivate about. He created this reaction by setting off a buzzer and simultaneously giving the dogs meat powder. The meat powder, of course, made the dogs salivate. After a while, they would salivate when the buzzer went off—even if the yummy powder failed to appear. If too much time went by without the powder being offered, however, the association between the sound and the treat wore off and the dogs no longer salivated when the buzzer was pushed.

People learn to be repelled by bias in exactly the same way that Pavlov's dogs learned to salivate at a sound. The only difference is that the dogs were conditioned by a positive reward (meat powder), while we are conditioned by a negative response (our parents' displeasure).

The chain reaction goes like this. As children, we say or do something inappropriate (the buzzer goes off), our parents react critically (the meat powder appears), and we feel negative about that action and the bias it reflects (we salivate). As with the dogs, after several associations between the two (the inappropriate action and our parents' displeasure), we begin to feel negatively about bias (salivate) even if our parents aren't around to provide their input.

If, however, the negative reaction—from our parents, other people, or the culture at large—does not continue with reasonable consistency to accompany events involving bias, we eventually become deconditioned and no longer wince at inappropriate jokes, comments, or actions. In short, we become insensitive to outrage (and the buzzer) and we no longer "salivate."

This is why it is our obligation to say something when a child—or anyone else—expresses a biased attitude. If the comment is met with a negative response, the speaker is more apt to see such statements as undesirable. It is also why bias cannot be tolerated from anyone, including women, people with disabilities, and members of emerging groups.

It is tempting to say, for example, that a woman's bias against other women doesn't count as much as a man's, or that a Chinese person's bias against the Japanese is OK because they are both Asian. This logic, however, crumbles when we realize that tolerating anyone's bias creates a climate in which the rest of us can feel that ours must be acceptable, too. When this happens, bias gradually becomes a transgression akin to cheating on one's taxes, and we begin to rationalize our prejudices by saying, "Everybody has biases, so why shouldn't I?"

It is also tempting to ignore biases of the Guerilla Bias variety and those containing positive characteristics. It is these, more than any, that float past us unnoticed, uncensored, and unremarked upon. If bias—any bias—is treated as somehow acceptable, if no one speaks up when it is voiced—no matter whose voice it is—the climate becomes compatible for its existence and for its spread.

CHAPTER SUMMARY

- Dialogue in the face of a Gateway Event is one of the most effective tools for reducing bias.
- Open and honest conversation reduces bias by increasing mutual knowledge and understanding.
- Honest dialogue about bias creates an atmosphere in which biases are unable to thrive.
- It is our obligation to speak up in the face of bias, no matter who holds it and no matter how benign that bias may seem.

12

GETTING DIVERSITY FIT

CHAPTER FOCUS QUESTION

How can I be prepared for a Gateway Event when it comes my way?

He couldn't call it anything other than an ambush or, if your taste runs to the medical, a "sudden onset" Gateway Event. It was early on a Monday morning and Wally was rushing to the weekly management meeting. Just as he rounded a corner, he practically collided with two of his supervisors, who were embroiled in a heated disagreement. As best he could figure it out, one of the combatants had offended the other with a comment about the new female sales associate. Knowing it was his job to do something, Wally stopped around the next turn, thought for a moment, and then, as if he had come to some kind of a decision, moved on down the hall. After all, he couldn't be late for his meeting. "I just couldn't handle it," he told me, "I was caught off guard and decided to let the incident pass."

Most Gateway Events are like this: They swing open before us without warning. We rarely have time to prepare a response or, for that matter, to sort out how we feel about what is going on. When this happens, we are in danger of walking away or, worse, going into autoresponder mode, spouting glib denials and politically correct nonsense. To prevent this kind of meltdown, we need to do what Wally did not do, which was to prepare ahead of time for every contingency.

Much of what you have read so far in this book amounts to that preparation: Becoming mindful of your biases, identifying their weak foundations, and learning to shove them aside are all part of your diversity fitness program. There is, however, one more workout that needs to be tackled to acquire—you guessed it—our desired "diversity hard body."

This exercise entails naming, and thus taming, the emotions that accompany Gateway Events. We have talked about emotion a lot in these pages, most notably the fears that animate and drive our biases. The emotions we are after here, however, are of a different sort. In this context, we are concerned with those small worries and larger fears that compromise in several ways our ability to carry on effective conversations about diversity and bias.

- Fear interferes with our willingness to enter into the conversation in the first place.
- Anxiety prevents us from being able to think on our feet.
- Agitation blocks our ability to interpret accurately what is going on.
- Fear pulls us out of the moment by tempting us to focus on painful experiences of the past or imagined disasters of the future rather than on the realities of the present.

If we are to be prepared to enter into gateway conversations and make them successful, we need to identify what we fear or, at the very least, what has us worried.

The ability to identify and observe an emotion is a cornerstone of emotional intelligence and greatly increases the chances of diminishing that emotion's impact on our ability to function.

The good news is that it isn't necessary to exorcise our fears and concerns altogether. Just identifying and naming them has a magical way of sapping their power.

I learned the importance of identifying my own fears some years ago, during a dinner with a new female acquaintance. Because my emotions were at that point still anonymous, they were utterly unchecked, cavorting around my mind in such a frenzy that they doomed what might have otherwise been a productive conversation. Here's the grizzly scene.

My dinner companion was a black woman named Candace, who had just moved to town and whom I was anxious to welcome into the community. We met at a local restaurant—a restaurant, in fact, owned by Deborah, the woman who so effectively educated her sexist, homophobic boss in an Chapter 11—and proceeded to have a great time indulging in "girl talk," being silly, comparing notes on the best shopping malls in town, and, most fun, trying to figure out how we were going to get her involved in the San Diego dating scene.

After about an hour of light conversation, we began to talk about my work and that led to what promised to be an interesting discussion about various types of diversity. Unfortunately, that promise was an empty one. Once the subject turned to race, there was a subtle shift in atmosphere. We were transformed into different people. Gone were the play and shared interests; we became, instead, a pair of women who were too self-conscious to carry on any kind of honest conversation. And the worst of it was that neither of us had the courage to so much as comment on what was happening between us.

Looking back, I realize that two stumbling blocks contributed to the broken promise of that evening—stumbling blocks that neither of us was able and/or willing to overcome. The first block was that we were clearly uncomfortable discussing the subject of race. Bruce Jacobs says that it requires more intimacy to talk honestly about race than to have sex.[1] That may be overstating it a bit, but talking about race sure is a heck of a lot scarier than chatting about shopping malls and clothes.

The second problem was actually the bigger one: the fact that neither of us had the courage to mention that the subject of race was making us uncomfortable. In short, neither of us was willing to acknowledge that we were jointly facing a Gateway Event. Because of our reluctance to state the obvious, we missed out on a prime opportunity to learn more about the complexities of human difference and how to make them work.

Why didn't at least one of us speak up? Why did we both refuse to enter into this Gateway Event? I wager it was fear or at least discomfort. But, what were we afraid of? If I had known that answer, at least from my end, I would have been able to explore the emotion and reduce its power. Maybe you have some insights into what was driving this conversational collapse.

Reader Exploration Point: Put yourself in my place or in Candace's—whichever role is most familiar to you (or both)—and try to identify what emotions kept each of us from walking bravely through that Gateway Event. In addition to speculating on the emotions that Candace and I may have felt, ask yourself what fears you might possess that could block your ability to pass smoothly through the next Gateway Event that comes your way.

Here are some of the feelings and fears that might have been responsible for that ruined dinner conversation:

- One emotion might have been fear of the intimacy (read honesty) and commitment that goes along with healthy conversation about diversity, related issues.
- There might also have been a concern that our own biases would be revealed if we carried the conversation forward. Perhaps Candace was concerned that, if we got into a really honest conversation, her bias toward white people would show through and damage a potential friendship. Perhaps I was worried that biases of which I was barely aware might make an inopportune appearance in the form of a misspoken word or poorly chosen phrase.
- Maybe one or both of us was afraid that the other person might become angry. Sadly, where there is diversity, there is always the possibility that old angers are festering just beneath the surface. Alternatively, we might have been worried that our own anger would leak through our reserve and spill out, ruining both the evening and the budding friendship.
- We might have been concerned about appearing uptight, judgmental, or overly serious. Often when a Gateway Event swings open before us, we reach out to slam it shut, for fear that if we bring up the heavy subject of diversity tension or bias, someone will hurl back at us that most patronizing of all phrases, "Lighten up!"

- Perhaps we were apprehensive that, if we said anything, we would give the impression of not being "nice people." Maybe neither of us wanted to be negative or confrontational in any way. Perhaps we feared that we would no longer be liked if we mentioned the harsh reality that our new friendship was not developing as smoothly as we had first expected and hoped.

One of the purposes of this book is to encourage you to walk through gateway after gateway and thus learn more and more about diversity, bias, and yourself. As you turn the handle on each gate, you will no doubt come up against fears and discomforts and other excuses to hesitate that are not on this list. The more experience you have in encountering, naming, and diffusing your fears, the easier the process will become. And the more prepared you will be to take on any Gateway Event that comes your way.

CHAPTER SUMMARY

- In order to participate successfully in Gateway Events, we need to name the fear, discomfort, or other emotion that prevents us from dialoguing effectively.
- Emotion not only makes us reluctant to talk about bias but also prevents us from thinking clearly, interpreting accurately what is going on, and focusing fully on the other participants in the conversation.
- The specific emotions that often accompany Gateway Events include discomfort with intimacy, fear of having our biases revealed, fear of our own or the other person's anger suddenly appearing, anxiety about being judged as excessively serious or uptight, and a concern with not being or appearing "nice."

CHAPTER

13

COGNITIVE SKILLS FOR DIVERSITY DIALOGUE

CHAPTER FOCUS QUESTION

What cognitive skills do I need in order to have an effective dialogue in the face of a Gateway Event?

Do any of these situations seem familiar?

- You are a manager who, during the weekly staff meeting you facilitate, hears one of your female team members accuse a colleague of sexism because of something he said. You heard his comment and think the woman is overreacting. What do you do?
- You are a CEO who just gave an important speech regarding goals for the next quarter. As you walk off the stage, one of your direct reports says she is offended by your comment that the company's new product would give the customer a real "bang for the buck." What do you do?
- You are a diversity manager who is conducting a pilot training program. Part of the course content deals with cultural differences in attitudes toward punctuality. In an attempt to contrast Latino notions of time with those found in mainstream U.S. culture, you refer to the latter as "normal," with the implication that Latino views are "abnormal." No one catches your faux pas. What do you do?

- You are a manager who is giving an important presentation to a group of your peers. Just as you begin to speak, you realize that there are two people in the audience who are deaf. You have not made arrangements for a signer. After the presentation, one of these participants comes up and complains. What do you do?
- You are an American whose parents immigrated to the United States from China. While standing in the computer room at work, you overhear someone tell a joke about a Chinaman, a priest, and a rabbi. What do you do?

If you think you know how to deal with these Gateway Events, you can skip right over this chapter. If, on the other hand, you look at each of these scenarios and get an uncomfortable feeling in the pit of your stomach and think, "Gosh, I'm sure glad that's never happened to me," you had best read on.

The purpose of this chapter is to provide the tools for turning your next Gateway Event from a relationship-ruining conflict into an opportunity for reduced bias and increased trust. Although Gateway Events come in many guises, I will focus the majority of this chapter on those dreadful moments when an utterance or an action has caused someone to feel offended. The skills offered here will apply whether you are the offended or the offender. As you read the chapter, keep in mind, however, that many of these skills are applicable to any situation involving diversity-related tension. The skills covered include:

- Resist the Urge to Jump to Conclusions
- Remember Past Experiences
- Set Productive Goals
- Recognize a Common Enemy
- Recognize Mutual Contributions to the Problem
- Practice the Pyramid Principle

RESIST THE URGE TO JUMP TO CONCLUSIONS

Despite all the regulations that clearly state "two pieces per passenger," the people boarding after me were laden with packages and bags and so-called carry-ons that seemed too large to take on the *Titanic* much less aboard a tiny regional jet. I was absorbed in my reading, so I didn't see it coming. Bam! This huge dark green duffel bag swung around and hit me, hard, in the head. I looked up and, with a scowl more appropriate to a deliberate attack than an act of clumsiness, struck back with an impatient, "Can't you be more careful?!" The woman who had lost control of the bag obviously had no intention of hitting me; nonetheless, my head hurt just as much as if it had been a carefully aimed assault—and my response was just as churlish.

My defensive reaction to this surprise attack is exactly what happens at the outset of many Gateway Events. This is especially true if what has collided with one's psyche is a comment or action that has offended us in some way. We initially recoil in surprise, and then lash out. What we don't do is take a moment to regroup and assess what is really going on. We may feel hurt or offended or angry. But no matter what the genre of discomfort, an ill-considered response will do more harm than good.

Most important, we need to do all we can to accurately assess the intent or attitude of the offender. Right about now, you might be asking some very pointed, and slightly testy, questions. "Who cares about intentions? If I'm hurt, that's all that matters." Of course the impact of an act matters, and that impact, if negative, must be remedied. The actor's intent, however, also needs to be taken into consideration, because knowledge of intent just might influence the success of that remedy.

The problem is, as Douglas Stone, Bruce Patton, and Sheila Heen say in their book *Difficult Conversations,* it is almost impossible to guess a person's intentions accurately.

Intentions are invisible. We assume them from other people's behavior. In other words, we make them up.[1]

We "make them up" largely according to the impact of the act on our welfare and, as we'll see shortly, according to our past experiences. Here's an example of how this can happen: A Latino family arrived at a high-end resort where they had long planned to spend their annual vacation. Upon checking in, they were given rooms far from the amenities of the property. When the family members saw the location of the rooms, they were disappointed and angry. Having been the targets of bias before, they jumped

Workplace Application: How Can You Tell What Action or Words Will Offend Others?

It is impossible to anticipate how every person will feel about a given action or comment. We can only do the best we can and use the tools and knowledge at our disposal. One of those tools is the ability to analyze our behaviors. Ask yourself the following questions, each of which is based on the premise that we fundamentally want to do the right thing:

1. Would I say or do this in front of my life partner, children, or respected friend? If the answer is no, you have established that you, at some level, know the action is inappropriate and potentially offensive.
2. Would I like it if a kinship group to which I belong were the recipient of a similar action or comment?
3. Have I done or said something like this before and, at the time, did it bother anyone?
4. Am I aware of other ways in which I have manifested what might be a biased attitude toward this group? If so, that bias could easily reveal itself in your comment or action.
5. Would I say or do this if a member of the group in question were within earshot? This is the real litmus test. If the answer is no, maybe not, or even I'm not sure, you are most certainly treading on dangerous ground.

to the conclusion that the hotel intended to discriminate against them. Ultimately, they sued.

What these guests didn't know was that they were given the remote location because that was the only way the hotel could accommodate their request for three connecting rooms; those were the only ones on the property. The hotel's intent was to accommodate their need, not to diminish them in any way. If they had resisted the urge to guess at intentions, a very nasty and expensive situation would have been avoided.

Here are some questions we can all ask ourselves the next time we feel that awful sense of hurt and anger that characterized this family's experience and that accompanies so many Gateway Events.

1. Is the offending word or action unusual for the person you are indicting? Of course, there is always a first time that a bias manifests itself in a behavior—just because it did not happen before does not rule out the possibility of bias. On the other hand, if the offending act is unusual, consider the possibility that the attitude behind the behavior was benign.
2. Has this person done other things that support your reaction or, on the contrary, has she demonstrated that she respects and cares about people who are different from herself?
3. If you have heard that she has done other things that might reflect a bias, are they merely rumors or are they events that you have witnessed and evaluated for yourself?

When we feel offended, the benefit of asking questions like these is enormous. That benefit is the acquisition of power. If we calmly examine what has happened, we gain the power that comes with objectivity. That power, in turn, grants us the option to either proceed confidently with our accusation or, alternatively, to shift our focus from the pain caused by the offense to the possibility of an unfortunate misunderstanding or an innocent act of clumsiness.

REMEMBER PAST EXPERIENCES

The Offender Remembers

Have you ever been accused of having a bias? This is no doubt one of the most distressing of Gateway Events. The pain, embarrassment, and self-doubt the event causes makes it almost impossible to think rationally, but think rationally we must.

Of course, just because someone makes an accusation of bias does not make him correct. Maybe there is a bias, maybe not. What it does mean, however, is that the offended party has been hurt and that hurt is real. It also means that he has handed you a gift. That gift is the opportunity and motivation to explore your own attitudes and find the truth. Ask yourself these questions:

1. Have I been accused of this particular bias before? Has it happened often? If the answer to these two questions is yes, you might have to face the painful reality that multiple people are not apt to be wrong. At the very least, it is time to look at the behaviors that have caused people to perceive you as biased. Even if others are mistaken about your attitude, there is something in your behavior that is making people uncomfortable.

2. Do I have a history of giving members of my own group a break? If the answer is yes, you might be guilty of what is called "leniency bias." Admittedly, leniency bias usually doesn't mean that you think your group is superior nor that you look down on others, but the negative consequence is the same as if you did: other groups are placed at a disadvantage.

3. When I am accused of bias, how long does it take me to recover from the initial feeling of defensiveness? The shorter the time, the better. It is, of course, natural to respond defensively to an accusation. The longer we hold that defensive stance, however, the greater the chance is that the accusation is correct. After all, if the bias weren't lurking in us somewhere, there'd be nothing to defend.

These questions, combined with the strategies outlined in Chapter 4 ("Become Mindful of Your Biases"), are powerful tools for uncovering unconscious bias or, to be more optimistic, revealing that you are innocent. In either case, you will know the truth of your motivations and be able to proceed with a conversation based on reality, not on a knee-jerk defensive response of the moment.

The Offended Remembers

Thinking back to past experiences is the responsibility not only of the offender, but also of the person at the receiving end of the offending action. Although the principle of examining past experiences is the same for both parties, there is one key difference. Whereas the person accused of bias looks back to assess the likelihood of a biased attitude, the person who has been hurt looks back to assess if maybe the offense she feels is a response to past experiences, rather than to the actions of the current offender.

Ask yourself whether the problematic act or word reminds you of past experiences with bias. If the answer is yes, then maybe, just maybe, you are responding to an earlier event, rather than to the current one. Perhaps the pain you feel is coming not, for example, from the vice president you believe denied your promotion because of your ethnicity, but from deep inside your own reservoir of unresolved slights and previous experience with bias.

James is a good example of how easy it is to fall into this trap. James, a gay man, has a reputation for accusing innocent colleagues of homophobia in the wake of the slightest transgressions on their part. James's subconscious doesn't care that most of the people in question don't have a homophobic bone in their bodies. To him, those individuals' innocence is irrelevant because others were guilty before them. Because he can't strike back at the true bigots who attacked him in the past—they are out of range—he goes after other parties who, although innocent, are closer at hand.

Frida, on the other hand, was successful at remembering the past when she encountered a potentially offending Gateway Event in her workplace. It happened when her boss—a man who had always treated her with great respect—made a point of mentioning Frida's Spanish language skills while introducing her to a new client. When he did this, she initially recoiled from the remark and found herself thinking something like, "What is he saying? Is he implying that he values me for my ethnicity alone?"

Frida was able, however, to immediately regroup from this initial reaction by remembering that she had heard similar comments in the past from people who did, in fact, devalue her. She knew it was those comments that were making her angry and suspicious; they had nothing to do with this man who gave every sign of appreciating Frida for all she had to offer.

SET PRODUCTIVE GOALS

How a Gateway Event resolves itself is predicated only in part on the details of the initial action. The ultimate outcome is also influenced by the sequence of decisions that follow. Arguably, the atrocity of September 11 was the largest Gateway Event in U.S. history. The flash points on that event, however, lay not only in the attack itself but in each subsequent reaction to it. In short, each swing of the gate following an event provides another opportunity to make good or bad choices, to set good or bad goals, and, therefore, to influence the outcome.

One such choice following September 11 was the sending of an angry e-mail to an Islamic Web site. That e-mail read, "Go back to your beautiful land of sand and pig dirt, and take your HATE with you." Not so good so far: a brutal attack (Gateway Event) followed by a response that had the potential to make matters worse. Fortunately, the recipient of that e-mail, Mohammed Abdul Aleem, possessed the courage and goodness to react with compassion and kind words. That kindness, that spin-off Gateway Event, had the desired effect of soliciting an equally compassionate response from the angry and, as it turns out, frightened American who had sent the initial e-mail. The man replied with this apology: "I was upset by all the things that happened. My brother lost several of his friends at the Pentagon. I appreciate your calm and informative response . . . and as a result have since then come to my senses."[2]

The difference between these two correspondents is that one reacted rashly to the initial incident (September 11) while the other took the time to decide what he wanted to accomplish with his response. The first man's goals were vague at best. Did he just want to vent his emotion? Did he actually want to create more animosity with his angry words? Did he have the conscious intention to motivate Mr. Aleem and his friends to go back to the Middle East? We don't know. But odds are pretty good that that frightened American, if asked, would say that he had no idea what he was trying to accomplish by what he did; he just did it. Mr. Aleem's goals, on the other hand, were clear: to restore communication and create goodwill.

This initially heated electronic exchange illustrates the profound importance of setting goals before entering into dialogue. Diversity consultant Roosevelt Thomas says it succinctly, but powerfully:

Dialogue is conversation with a purpose.[3]

Aimless conversation, particularly if the catalyst for that conversation is emotionally charged, will lead nowhere or, worse, will lead somewhere we would rather not go. We need functional dialogue about bias, not just noise, and certainly not just conflict for conflict's sake.

Your specific goal or function will, of course, be shaped by the nature of the Gateway Event itself. The following is a sampling of the kinds of events you are most apt to encounter, along with suggested goals. Keep this discussion in mind so that, when each situation presents itself, you will be prepared and able to enter into the dialogue with a firm function in mind.

You Feel Offended—What Is Your Goal?

When someone has done something we find offensive, it is our task and responsibility to communicate how we feel, in a way that will accomplish our goals. I doubt it, but your goal might be to upset the person, make him feel guilty, and hurt him (like so many like him have hurt you before). Let's admit it, there is a certain pleasure in making people feel guilty. The problem is that guilt-tripping is a notoriously poor motivator of change. A little guilt served up gently might work, but too much can backfire and that backfire inevitably ignites a circle of destruction that spins out of control:

- The circle starts when a statement or act is perceived by someone as offensive.
- The person who feels hurt accuses the offender of bias and then says something with the goal of making him feel guilty.
- The guilt-tripped offender dislikes the accuser for making him feel guilty and, therefore, withdraws and becomes belligerent.
- The accuser perceives this belligerence as still more reason to be offended and redoubles her efforts to make the offender feel guilty.
- The offender (who, by the way, is rapidly taking on the role of victim) again withdraws.
- The accuser perceives this withdrawal as . . .

I told you the circle would spin; even my head is spinning from trying to figure out how all this jousting works. Setting the goals of guilt and revenge doesn't seem like a very good idea to me.

My friend Barbara Ceconi, whom you met earlier, was, she admits, once tempted to go down the rocky road to revenge. This urge occurred when she encountered a man on the street who found it entertaining—or felt it was his moral obligation or some other such foolishness—to call her a lesbian. Barbara, as you know, is blind and was walking with a female friend, who was guiding her by the arm. As the man walked past the pair, Barbara heard him mutter, "Look at those lesbians flaunting their homosexuality. It's disgusting."

When Barbara heard this barely audible attack, she had a choice to make and a goal to set. Barbara's chosen goal would depend on the answer to two questions.

1. What did she want to accomplish?
2. Was there a reasonable chance of her achieving that goal without paying too high a price? In other words, was it worth it?

One goal Barbara might have had is a sometimes sweet one: revenge. Imagine his humiliation at being accosted in public by a blind woman and berated for calling her disgusting. If Barbara wanted to feel better by causing pain, this certainly was achievable. But it also would compromise a more important long-term goal: to educate others about how people with disabilities should be regarded and treated.

It is impossible to know if Barbara could have succeeded at educating this particular person—that would have been determined by the nature of the man and the virulence of his fear. Her odds for success, however, would have soared if she approached him with compassion and with the intent of preserving both her dignity and his. Knowing what I do of Barbara, that is just how she would have gone about it. Barbara knows that people are far more apt to listen if they are not distracted by efforts to build an emotional firewall with which to protect themselves against attack.

Reader Exploration Point: Think back to a time when you were offended by someone's comment or action. What goal did you set for the conversation that followed? Having read this section, what goals might you set for the future?

You Have Done Something Offensive and Now Regret It—What Is Your Goal?

If most of us were to answer this question honestly, we might say, "My goal is to make the whole thing go away." Of course, that's not going to work. For one thing, it's impossible. For another, all our efforts to ignore it, make a joke out of it, or just walk away from it are disrespectful and—let's face it—cowardly. I remember a moment some years ago when I said something offensive, knew it, felt awful about it, and set for myself the unrecommended goal of trying to make everyone, including myself, believe it never happened.

The unfortunate event took place when my children were teenagers, some 20 years ago. I was standing at my kitchen counter next to one of my daughter's best friends—a young man who, by heritage, was part Japanese. As odd as it may sound to those who know of my lack of culinary skills, I have the vague impression that he and I were cooking together. Well, maybe the "cooking" was more along the lines of unwrapping some take-out food or maybe as sophisticated as slicing a pizza. Anyway, for a reason I can't recall, I had occasion to refer to Asian food and, somewhere in there, I uttered the phrase, "Ching Chong food."

As soon as the phrase left my mouth, I regretted it. He didn't say anything, but there was this nanosecond of silence that screamed embarrassment and hurt feelings and discomfort. You might have expected that I would take advantage of that gap in the banter to apologize, but I didn't—no excuse for that, just too buried in my own regret to do the right thing. My goal that afternoon, standing in my kitchen, was obvious: Make it go away. A better goal, of course, would have been for me to do anything it took to make him feel less diminished by what I had said. That means, acknowledge what happened, take responsibility for it, and apologize.

By the way, with respect to this young man, I very recently remembered this event and, with the clarity of thought and courage that intervening years can supply, was able to shift my goal from "hide it" to "fix it." After all these years, I tracked him down and apologized.

You Have Been Wrongly Accused of Bias—What Is Your Goal?

Let's say you have been accused of a bias. You really listened to what the other person had to say, really thought it out, and are convinced that the accusation is wrong. What on earth is your goal then? I can best answer this question by telling you what happened to my colleague

Gayle who is, as you can see from this incident, very skilled at handling awkward Gateway Events.

> Gayle, an experienced diversity trainer, was about halfway through conducting a workshop when he had occasion to refer to the "flip" chart that stood in the corner of the room. No sooner was the word out of his mouth that a hand shot up. "How can you, a diversity trainer, be so biased? 'Flip,'" the irate woman said, "is a pejorative term for Filipinos."

Yes, *flip* is a pejorative term for Filipinos. But it is also the name of a large pad of paper mounted on an easel. Gayle would agree with me that this woman's reasoning—that an offensive word is a reflection of bias even if it is used for an entirely different purpose—was a bit off base. If we carry her thinking to its logical conclusion, a woman would be right to protest every reference to baby "chicks." People of Asian ancestry could become angry when the "slope" of an incline is mentioned. And a person with a disability might express outrage when hearing a golfer refer to his "handicap."

Faced with such distorted reasoning, Gayle had a couple of options. He could set a goal of making the accuser feel justified (and end up looking like a good guy in the deal). To accomplish this, he would have to pretend that the accusation was correct and fake an apology (that means, lie). A corollary result of this misguided goal would be that the accuser would remain ignorant of her mistake and continue to chronically see bias where none exists.

On the other hand, he could set this goal:

> *Demonstrate to the woman that he respects her enough to hold her to a high standard of judgment.*

This is exactly what Gayle did. First, he thanked the woman for her comment and said he was sorry if what he said made her uncomfortable. This was an important step because it made it clear that he honored her right to feel the way she did. Notice a distinction here: Gayle did not actually apologize for using the word *flip;* he apologized, instead, for the fact that his use of the word made her uncomfortable. This nuanced apology was one step toward his goal of showing her respect. In short, he resisted the temptation to patronize her.

The second step toward his goal grows from Gayle's assumption that the woman would be able to understand the distinction he was making in what the word *flip* actually means—no Guerilla Bias here. He respectfully pointed out that the term "flip," in the context in which he used the term, meant only a large pad of paper and nothing else. He then went a step further and asked the woman if she'd like to talk about the issue more during the break—another sign of respect.

Reader Exploration Point: Think back to a time when you were falsely accused of a biased attitude. Upon learning of that accusation, what, if any, goal did you set for the conversation? Having read this section, what goal might you set if a similar incident happened in the future?

RECOGNIZE A COMMON ENEMY

It was the night of the Los Angeles riots, April 1992. I lived in San Diego but was vividly aware of the chaos that reigned 135 miles up the coast. Between phone calls from frenzied relatives and the lurid television coverage, it seemed that my childhood hometown had turned into an inferno of hatred and violence. Finally, it all got to be too much, so my husband and I decided to drive down to the local mall in a futile effort to escape reality.

The mall was deserted except for a few other couples who, like us, were ambling from shop window to shop window. I recall one couple in particular. The only reason I remember them is the color of their skin—and that color was black. As we passed within a few feet of each other, I swear there was unspoken communication between us. My silent contribution to the conversation were questions like, "Do you think I'm racist because I'm white?" "Are you angry with me too?" "Do you think I'm afraid of you?" Their questions were, "Do you hate me for what is going on in LA?" "Are you afraid of me?" "Are you resentful of me and the color of my skin?"

Workplace Application: Time to Talk

Learning from others is a valuable means of gaining skill in handling Gateway Events. For this reason, it is suggested that you create a permanent agenda item at your regularly scheduled management meetings during which incidents of diversity-related tension are addressed. Specifically, invite any team member who has had a recent Gateway Event to discuss these questions:

1. What were the details of the incident?
2. What did you or the other people involved do right to resolve the event?
3. What did you or the other people involved do wrong?

Invite the group to suggest how the event might have been handled better and/or to ask questions about similar situations they might currently be experiencing.

How wonderful it would have been had we been able—I should say, willing—to approach one another and ask these questions out loud. Had we done so, we would have discovered that we shared something very profound: a common foe.

In every situation in which there is conflict around difference, there is, by definition, a common enemy, and that enemy is a shared culture of bias that tricks and seduces us into misunderstanding and mistrust. No matter what genre of Gateway Event might bring us into a conversation about bias, no matter how different we seem and how separate our stances, we share the sad reality that we have all been injured by the same adversary. Some of us have injuries more severe than others. Some have fatal wounds, some mere contusions. But, no matter what the degree . . .

We have all been damaged by the existence of bias in our culture.

Perhaps you are damaged because of disadvantages resulting from your gender or sexual orientation. Perhaps you have had little bias directed against you, but are a victim just the same because your own biases have deprived you of rich relationships and fruitful experiences. Maybe you are a victim because the prevalence of bias has led to false accusations against you. Or maybe you are an innocent bystander caught in a crossfire of fear and conflict. No matter who we are and no matter what our perspective, bias is an enemy we all share. The more we shift our emphasis during conversations from fighting each other to fighting the common foe, the more productive those conversations will become.

Candace and I should have done this. As I think back, our shared enemy was right there, perched on the bar stool next to us, whispering historical truisms artfully interspersed with lies and distortions, creating fear, and hesitation, and distrust. If only we had had the presence of mind to call out the enemy, to name her, and to say to each other, "Wow, isn't this weird? Before we began talking about race, we were having fun. Now that the subject has come up, we're all self-conscious and tongue-tied. I wonder what's going on?"

Candace and I, two intelligent and educated women, could have out-matched the demon, but we allowed the foe to divide us, and that was our fatal mistake. We were both prisoners of the bias wars, under siege in the same stone fortress, listening to the same propaganda. Rather than recognize that reality and join our skills to concoct an escape plan, we essentially fought each other. Tony and Dennis didn't make that mistake; they identified the enemy, stood on each other's shoulders, and scaled the wall to freedom.

RECOGNIZE MUTUAL CONTRIBUTIONS TO THE PROBLEM

Every Gateway Event is a collaborative effort. One of the parties might hold the moral high ground and be more "right" than the other, but both people, by virtue of the fact that they are present, must in some way have contributed to the friction. Notice that I say "contributed"; this has nothing to do with blame, guilt or innocence, or with who should rightfully be punished. If I leave my purse on the front porch and someone takes it, I am certainly not to blame, but my absentmindedness was a contributing factor to the fact that the bag was stolen.

Here is an example of how two people contributed to a Gateway Event that might have turned ugly. It started when a woman named Nonna accused Rachel, her manager, of bias against her and the other Russian immigrants in the department. When Rachel heard the accusation, she was initially shocked. After talking to Nonna, however, she realized that they shared equal responsibility for the negative feeling between them.

As it turns out, Nonna, since arriving in the United States, had experienced discrimination at every turn. Because of these bad experiences, she developed the habit of seeing bias even where none existed. For her part, Rachel tended to stay to herself, rarely mixed with her colleagues, and never socialized with them outside of work. On top of that, she admitted to having difficulty understanding her Russian-born team members' accents and, because she was uncomfortable, avoided having conversations on the plant floor.

Between Rachel's natural coolness and Nonna's sensitivity to perceived bias, it is no wonder there was tension. This is a case of two women, both innocent, and yet both contributors to a tension that could have proved painful and expensive.

Obviously, an important element in any good conversation following a Gateway Event is the willingness to admit your own contribution. This means being self-aware and honest. Here are some examples of the kinds of admissions that will guarantee a more productive dialogue.

- If you have contributed to a Gateway Event by accusing someone of sexism, admit you tend to see sexism a lot because of past experiences. This admission does not automatically mean your accusation is wrong; it does, however, communicate your willingness to talk honestly and openly.
- If someone has accused you of bias against people over 60, admit you grew up slightly afraid of older people and still might not be completely free of that feeling. Again, this admission does not automatically mean you are guilty, only that you are aware and take ownership of past influences on your thinking.
- If someone has expressed concern about your attitude toward people who are gay, admit that you may have contributed to that perception because you are a little uncomfortable with those who have a different sexual orientation than your own. This is not an admission of homophobia, only a sign of your willingness to explore the issue from all angles.

We need to acknowledge our contribution at every opportunity. Sure, every once in a while, the other person will take our inch of admission and stretch it into a distorted mile in which the truth is hardly recognizable or, worse, will use it as a shield to keep from seeing her own role in the event. Usually, however, people will respond positively to the gift of your vulnerability and, in turn, become more willing to look at, and confess to, their own share of responsibility.

Reader Exploration Point: Included here is an event containing mutual contributions to a Gateway Event. On the basis of the details provided, can you identify the role that Cindy and Horace each played in creating this situation?: Cindy, president of a largely female-staffed cosmetics firm, failed to invite Horace, her new administrative assistant, to the weekly board meeting. Not realizing that it had always been Cindy's policy to exclude support staff from these meetings, Horace complained of sexism and unfair treatment.

Here are some thoughts on Cindy's and Horace's mutual contributions to the problem.

- Cindy has the right to exclude anyone she wants from her meetings. The fact that she didn't include Horace is, nonetheless, a contributing factor to the situation.
- Cindy further contributed by failing to tell Horace of her policy about who does and does not attend board meetings.
- Horace, on the other hand, contributed by jumping to a conclusion about Cindy's motivation; he never even considered asking why he had been excluded.

Again, there is no blame here, no bad guy, just two people who, through a series of decisions and actions, contributed to what might have been a very sticky Gateway Event.

PRACTICE THE PYRAMID PRINCIPLE

It was February 2006 when I sat in my hotel room in Cairo, feet up on the sill, whiskey glass in hand, gazing out the window at one of the most amazing sights on the planet: the Great Pyramid of Cheops. Looming in the mist, it seemed grander and more elegant than its likeness in even the most touched-up travel photograph.

I wasn't thinking much about bias reduction on that romantic night, but the image of the pyramid stayed with me and laid the foundation for what I call the Pyramid Principle for succeeding at gateway conversations. This strategy is informed by what any architect knows about building: whether constructing the Pyramid of Cheops, Blenheim Palace, the Vatican, or the Great Wall of China, the only way to proceed is one stone at a time.

When it comes to conversations about bias, this means we need to adopt a helpful motto.

"Think small."

Often, in the heat of a Gateway Event, we become overloaded by the scope of the issue and the intensity of emotion. That overload can, in turn, leave us paralyzed and unable to act. The trick to popping the clutch and getting moving again is to sidestep the main issue of the conflict for a moment—don't worry, we'll get back to it later—and, instead, build a foundation of small successes on which the solution to the big problem can ultimately rest. By thinking smaller, we create bite-size strategies that can be swallowed without gagging and that are manageable even when we are lost in a maze of self-consciousness, anger, or fear.

Looking back on my ill-fated lunch with the Harvard graduate (Chapter 11), I realize I could have used the Pyramid Principle to make progress toward better communication with this fascinating young man. There was no way that we were going to leap to mutual understanding and trust in the span of one Cobb salad and a lemonade, but we could have taken a few tentative steps in that direction.

For one thing, we might have admitted our discomfort and thereby cracked open the door to better dialogue: Stone Number One.

We then might have agreed to take turns talking for short periods without interruption or reprisal from the other: Stone Number Two.

We might also have made a pact that, should one person not understand something, he or she would ask for clarification: Stone Number Three.

We might have worked to find one thing to agree on. This might have been one small fact, one goal, or one emotion: Stone Number Four.

And wider and wider the base becomes, and firmer the foundation, until we have constructed, if not the Great Pyramid of Cheops, at least a modest structure of good communication with the potential of better understanding.

CHAPTER SUMMARY

- Resist the urge to jump to conclusions about the intent or attitude of someone who has offended you. The impact of that offense matters, but so does intent, as it dictates how best to resolve the situation.
- If someone has accused you of bias, look into your past to see if this has happened before. If so, the accusation just might be correct.
- If someone has offended you, consider the possibility that you are reacting to past experiences with bias, rather than to the current offender.
- Setting goals before entering into a Gateway Event increases the chances of achicving a positive outcome.
- All parties to a Gateway Event share—to some degree and in some way—bias as a common enemy.
- Gateway conversations are more apt to end successfully if we recognize the contributions of all participants.
- Gateway Events are best resolved by breaking the problem and the solution into small, easily managed units.

CHAPTER

14

VERBAL SKILLS FOR DIVERSITY DIALOGUE

CHAPTER FOCUS QUESTION

What verbal skills do I need in order to have an effective dialogue in the face of a Gateway Event?

Pee Wee Reese, captain of the Brooklyn Dodgers in the 1940s and 1950s, knew nothing about the rules of political correctness the day he faced an angry crowd on a baseball field in Louisville, Kentucky. Despite a lack of sophistication and his being a child of the times, Pee Wee's language was one of highest respect and compassion. As taunts of "Jungle Bunny" hurled down on Jackie Robinson, Pee Wee quietly walked from his position at shortstop and put an arm around Jackie's shoulder. Pee Wee, a slight man, a white man, and a southerner, said not one word. His elegant gesture permeated and diluted the climate of hatred more effectively than the most effusive of tirades. Jackie, by the way, got the message, too. His response? "I never felt alone on a baseball field again."[1]

Pee Wee's eloquence had nothing to do with using the latest terminology or most precise pronoun. Pee Wee was a good communicator. He was a good communicator because he knew his audience, and he knew that rhetorical overkill would only make this Gateway Event spiral down into a morass of racial hatred and violence. He also knew that the language chosen needed to be simple: an arm around the shoulder. Enough said.

The purpose of this chapter is to help us all learn to communicate as eloquently as Pee Wee Reese. In the last two chapters, we focused on the cognitive and emotional skills we need to reach that goal. In this chapter, we will turn our attention to the words themselves—which ones to choose and how they should be spoken.

- Modulate Your Voice and Your Words
- Avoid Dogmatic and Dismissive Language
- Use Creative Communication Strategies
- Listen, Listen, Listen

MODULATE YOUR VOICE AND YOUR WORDS

The communication principle that Pee Wee understood more than any other is the importance of modulation. In radio, modulation means to adjust the phase, frequency, or amplitude of a transmission to a level that will most successfully carry the broadcast. In human communication, and no more so than in the emotionally charged context of Gateway Events, modulation means to lower our verbal and vocal volume to ensure that our message is heard. Pee Wee carried this advice one step further and essentially "modulated" his body language by making a simple, gentle, and quiet gesture that effectively diffused his and Jackie Robinson's Gateway Event.

Vocal Modulation

My father, who was an actor, taught me something important about the presentation of dialogue, ideas, or accusations.

Lower your voice.

By softening our voice, we allow, and even tempt, the listener to crane forward to hear, and more readily understand, what this mysterious and barely audible message is all about. As my father used to say, "A whisper is more tantalizing and a lot more interesting than a shout." While loud and harsh utterances cause most of us to retreat behind a soundproof wall of denial and disinterest, a softer tone has a remarkable way of creating a feeling of safety for—and, therefore, receptivity in—the listener.

Verbal Modulation

This lowering of "volume" applies not just to how loud we speak but also to the intensity of the words we use. Admittedly, verbal modulation is tough for many Americans because our culture loves large language. We like to indulge in a kind of overspeak in which every book is "best-selling," every news story "breaking," and the latest comedies inevitably "hilarious." This is all very nice when pitching a product or getting someone to buy your newspaper. Exaggeration, however, is a surefire way to draw psychological blood—inflaming the dialogue to the point of conflagration or, worse, shutting the conversation down entirely.

Many of us believe that for words to be effective, they must be forceful, dramatic, and exaggerated. The opposite is true.

Understatement is almost always more powerful, and often more accurate, than exaggeration.

Assume for the moment that someone has offended you and your goal is to help reduce any bias he may have—or, at the very least, motivate him to stop and think next time around. You will have a far better chance of accomplishing this goal if you avoid using exaggerated terms or what is referred to as hyperbole.

Unfortunately, anger and stress tempt us to use potent verbiage like *racist, sexist,* and *homophobic. Homophobic,* for example, is a clinical term meaning "a pathological obsession with homosexuality caused by the heavily suppressed fear that one may be homosexual oneself." Wouldn't you agree that a "pathological obsession" is absurd hyperbole when applied to Lilly's office mate whose "obsession" went no further than to express surprise that Lilly was gay? We accomplish only one thing when we spread such potent words around so liberally: we weaken the impact of our message.

Another problem with the use of hyperbole is that it gives the accused justification to play the innocent. Most people associate words such as *racist* with blatant discrimination, *homophobic* with hate crimes, and *sexist* with the desire to keep women barefoot and pregnant. "That's not me," the defendant is apt to think with relief. And most of the time, if measured by what those words traditionally mean, he'll be right. If, on the other hand, the terms of attack were more reasoned, if the crime of which we accuse someone were pled down to a misdemeanor, then maybe we could maintain an atmosphere in which a productive conversation could take place. Psychologist Paul Wachtel addresses a related idea in *Race in the Mind of America.*

> Accusing a guilty man of the wrong crime is one of the greatest gifts one can bestow upon him. It fosters an orgy of self-righteous conviction of innocence, and conveniently diverts his attention from the offense of which he is truly guilty.[2]

Cranking up the emotional volume, which is what hyperbole is all about, provides no assurance that your message will be heard. It instead guarantees that the accused, whether guilty or innocent, will be sorely tempted to cover her ears, learn nothing, and turn and walk away.

A much better way to express our complaint is to couch it in terms of behaviors and feelings, rather than labels. Here are two approaches to the same Gateway Event. Read them over and see which one you think is more apt to achieve the dual goals of good communication and behavior change:

1. *Approach A:* Sophie, having worked for months with a boss who treated her poorly, walked into his office, sat down, and said, "I'm really tired of your sexist treatment. You ignore my ideas, never give me feedback, and regularly exclude me from key meetings. Your bias against women will have to change, or I'll have no choice but to go to human resources with a complaint."

2. *Approach B:* Sophie, having worked for months with a boss who treated her poorly, walked into his office, sat down, and said, "I need to let you know what I have been experiencing. Very often I find myself feeling ignored, and I really do need more feedback on how I am doing. Also, it would be helpful to my career if I could attend more of the management meetings. To be honest, I am very concerned about this."

I'm going to assume that you agree with me that Approach B is far more likely than A is to change the behavior of Sophie's boss, and maybe even his attitude. The biggest problem with Approach A is that, in that scenario, Sophie labels her boss's behavior and makes assumptions about his attitude and intentions—he is, she has decided, sexist and biased. Of course it is possible that he does have these attitudes. But Sophie can't know that for sure. Because she doesn't know for sure, there is no point in her using the labels. All her use of labels is apt to accomplish is to make her boss defensive and angry. Sophie's goal of changing his behavior would be better served by sticking to the facts that have been proved. She is uncomfortable and dissatisfied. Period.

The Sophie we meet in the second approach does just that; she talks not about what he is doing or what his attitude may or may not be but about how it is affecting her. The fundamental reason Approach B is so effective is that it avoids giving the boss a reason to become defensive. No labeling, no insults, and no threats. This approach is far more apt to allow him to stay receptive to what she has to say. Who knows, he might just hear her and decide to make some changes.

AVOID DOGMATIC AND DISMISSIVE LANGUAGE

Another language choice that can interfere with our conversational goals is the use of dogmatic or absolute statements. Have you ever been in a discussion in which one person rebuts an argument with, "That's the way everybody does it," or, "That's what I was taught," or, "Well, that's just the way it is"? Statements like these serve little purpose other than to shut down the conversation and any learning that might have taken place.

Of course, we have every right to believe in majority rule or in what our parents taught us. What we don't have is the right to use these beliefs as devices to stop dialogue. Slamming the ideological lid on a topic might make us feel righteous and safe, but it is also an excellent way to defeat our goals of sustaining productive conversation, getting to know each other better, and pounding another nail into the coffin of bias.

It is when someone has accused us of a biased attitude that we are most tempted to make dogmatic statements. Particularly if we haven't gotten ourselves diversity fit, we are apt to buckle at the knees and at the heart, and lash back with an inflexible, "You're too sensitive," or that pair of old standbys, "You know what I meant" and "I was only kidding." Each of these dismissive phrases does little more than make the object of the allegedly offending statement feel still more diminished and the person who has been accused of bias look foolish and unkind.

Gayle, no doubt, would have studiously avoided all these phrases. You recall from the last chapter that he is the one who was accused of bias for using the term *flip* during a training session. After respectfully explaining the context in which he used the word, Gayle invited his accuser to discuss the issue during a break. Although we are not privy to that conversation, my guess is that Gayle resisted the urge to make any inflexible statements that would have served only to stop the discussion and make himself appear defensive.

Reader Exploration Pont: Put yourself in Gayle's position. What phrases might Gayle have used during the conversation?

Had we been eavesdropping, we might have heard Gayle say things like the following:

- "You have a different perspective. I'd like to hear more."
- "Thanks for speaking up about how you feel. We need more open discussions like this."
- "I can't honestly say I agree with you, but I'd sure like to talk about it some more."

Admittedly, open-ended, nondogmatic statements and questions like these do take a little courage to utter. That is because they just might produce a rich conversation in which honest emotions and ideas are exchanged— kind of scary, but very much worth the risk.

USE CREATIVE COMMUNICATION STRATEGIES

Creative Ways to Use Analogies

Often the issues we are dealing with in Gateway Events are complex and confusing. Because of this complexity, our language needs to be clear, and it needs to be language to which the other person can relate. An analogy, for example, is a great tool for helping someone grasp, and even agree with, your point of view.

I learned this technique during a mild Gateway Event involving my husband and myself. It happened when I realized that Tom was failing to grasp why having the Confederate flag flying over the South Carolina courthouse was upsetting to some black Americans. He just couldn't get it. He kept coming back at me with arguments like, "But, the flag symbolizes more than just slavery," "It was so long ago," and, "What about the people who value the good part of southern culture? Don't they get to have their flag?" Finally, I realized I needed to talk about this issue in terms that connected to one of Tom's kinship groups, his Swedish heritage. Here's my side of the conversation.

> Tom, assume for the moment that the Swedes were enslaved by the Norwegians until the middle of the 19th century. Also assume that, during that time, the Norwegians had a flag symbolizing their beliefs that they had the right to own slaves and that Norwegians were innately superior to Swedes. Eventually, let's say, the Norwegians were forced by the Danes to free the Swedes, but continued to use the flag as a symbol of their history and identity. Now, how would you feel about seeing that symbol on the top of your own government buildings?

Need I say more? Tom got it.

Creative Ways to Redirect the Conversation

Another way to communicate creatively is to redirect a person's thinking. Take a look at how Zack skitters away from facing his Guerilla Bias and how Grace smoothly redirects his attention to the main point of the conversation:

> Grace calls Zack into her office because of her concern about the uneven feedback he is giving his team members. According to what she has heard, Zack is great at telling the older employees where they need to improve, but he completely neglects the errors made by Josie, a 22-year-old who has only been with the company

a few months. When Grace asks Zack if this is true, he says, "You bet it is. My goal is to treat everyone fairly. Josie is so young, I want to be careful not to discourage her this early in her career."

Despite Grace's surprise at this blatant display of Guerilla Bias, she responds appropriately by saying, "I appreciate your trying to be fair, but don't you see that your lack of feedback means Josie won't know where to improve?" Zack misses the point and responds with, "That's OK, she'll never know that I am treating her differently—she'll just think she is doing a good job."

Here are two ways in which Grace might answer Zack. Which one do you think is best?

1. *Option I:* Respond as if his statement about her never finding out is the point and say, "But, Zack, what if she finds out one day? She is apt to be very upset."

2. *Option II:* Call him on his attitude and say, "It doesn't matter whether or not she ever finds out. In our workplace, we treat everyone with respect and not coaching her properly is disrespectful."

Option II is the better solution. Do you see the difference? The first approach does nothing to move Zack ahead in his bias-awareness process. It also reinforces his faulty thinking ("She'll never know") and sends the message that secrecy within the department can be tolerated. Grace instead redirected the conversation to the real issue: the negative impact of Zack's behavior on Josie. At the same time, she was able to reinforce the value of communicating respect for all employees. We, of course, can't be sure if this strategy eroded Zack's Guerilla Bias, but it sure was a heck of a first step.

LISTEN, LISTEN, LISTEN

Booker Izell, formerly vice president of diversity at the *Atlanta Journal,* has much to teach us about how to dialogue about diversity and the power that such dialogue has for reducing bias. Booker travels a great deal, and one day he had the misfortune—or at least it initially looked like a misfortune—to sit next to a deeply biased man on an airplane:

Upset by an article he had just read about crime in the black community, the man turned to Booker and said something about blacks acting like animals. Sensing a Gateway Event in the offing and keeping his cool, Booker responded with, "You do know I'm black, don't you?" Undeterred and remarkably unembarrassed, the seatmate said, "Oh, you're OK, but I think we should send the bad ones back to Africa."

The man was talking so loudly that the flight attendant became concerned and offered Booker another seat. Much to her surprise, and certainly to the surprise of Booker's seatmate, he refused the attendant's offer, saying, "I want to hear this. I want to listen to his point of view." The two men talked for the entire length of the flight. After they landed and retrieved their carry-on luggage from the overhead rack, the man reached out to shake Booker's hand and said, "I enjoyed talking to you. I can't promise that I'll change, but you really have given me food for thought."

Booker, and his willingness to listen, just may have started this man down the road to something good. Booker knew how to listen; he knew that listening means to stay present—in the moment—listening only to the person in front of you. This wasn't easy for him because dozens, if not hundreds, of other white men were horning in on this mile-high conversation. Those interlopers were the racist men who had previously made Booker feel small and "less than" and diminished because of his color. But Booker had the moral strength to exclude these others from the dialogue and listen only to the one human being who sat beside him.

Judging from the success of this conversation, I would bet that Booker abided by another cardinal rule of good listening:

No "cross talk" allowed.

Cross talk is a term used at Alcoholics Anonymous meetings and refers to the rule that allows each person to talk without interruption or rebuttal. By refraining from cross talk, the full breadth of the speaker's thoughts and emotions can be laid on the table.

I used to do this with my daughter. We had a ritual in which she or I invited the other to indulge in a good "vent." This meant allowing an unbroken stream of emotion and words to pour out without criticism or response. Venting sessions like these encourage and allow emotions to be expressed. And when it comes to reducing bias, understanding emotions is crucial. As the authors of *Difficult Conversations* point out, if you don't listen to emotions, "you'll get the plot, but not the point."[3]

Unfortunately, when we talk about something that involves a difference of opinion, as is the case with most Gateway Events, we tend not to listen. This is because we believe that really listening gives the impression that we agree with our opponent. In fact, eloquent listening sends only one message: that we care about resolving the situation. George, Charmaine's boss, delivered this message at a time when she desperately needed to hear it:

> When Charmaine was passed over for a promotion, she went to George and accused him of homophobia. At the start of the conversation, she was very emotional, not just because of the loss of this one promotion, but also because she had recently been the victim of two layoffs. She felt vulnerable, abused, and a little frightened. As Charmaine talked, George knew her charges were false; nonetheless, he fell silent and listened. When she was finished, he understood how frustrated she was and why she might have mistaken workplace realities for discrimination.

If George had refused to listen, if he had succumbed to anger or defensiveness and had begun to jabber on about how wrong Charmaine was, he never would have gained that understanding. As it was, he was able to empathize with her frustrations, explain the situation, avoid costly litigation, and retain a valuable employee to boot.

CONCLUSION: LIVING ANYWHERE WE WANT

Obviously, Tony and Dennis didn't need any of the techniques discussed in these last three chapters. Good conversation came naturally to them. It has been 50 years since that first encounter in college, and they are still friends. Dennis, in fact, writes Tony often and teases him with the

Guidelines to Productive Dialogue

The following responses are merely guidelines. They are to be used as a starting point for phrasing and verbiage that reflect your individual personality and your relationship to the person with whom you are speaking.

1. **The Situation:** A colleague has approached you to say that something you said was offensive to him. When you hear what he has to say, you realize your mistake.

    Unproductive Response: Not wanting to admit you are wrong, you say, "How can you say that? You knew I was only kidding." (The Problem with This Response: It is dishonest in that you really do know that you are wrong. Also, it negates your colleague's feelings and shuts down dialogue.)

    Productive Response: "I'd never have known what I did if you hadn't told me. Thanks so much for being so open; I'm really sorry I said what I did." (The Advantage of This Response: It communicates respect for the other person and promotes continued dialogue.)

2. **The Situation:** A woman on your team tells you that you did something at the last management meeting that she found deeply offensive. You don't understand what, if anything, you have done wrong. You suspect there has been a misunderstanding.

    Unproductive Response: "I'm so sorry I did that. Please forgive me." (The Problem with This Response: It is dishonest and patronizing in that you are not at all sure you have actually done anything wrong. Also, this false apology implies that you believe the other person incapable of having an honest discussion about the issue.)

    Productive Response: "I'll admit I'm a little thrown by this and can't honestly say I understand, but I sure do apologize if something I did made you uncomfortable. Can we talk about it some more?" (The Advantage of This Response: It is honest. It honors the accuser's right to feel as she does and communicates respect for her ability to engage in honest conversation.)

(continued)

3. **The Situation:** You have just said something inappropriate or offensive. You realize it, but no one else seems to have noticed.

   Unproductive Response: You say nothing in the hope that no one will notice your mistake. (The Problem with This Response: By not saying anything, you miss an opportunity to demonstrate respect for those whom you might have offended.)

   Productive Response: "Did anybody catch what I just said? I really apologize." (The Advantage of This Response: It demonstrates respect and models the importance of being open and courageous around diversity issues.)

4. **The Situation:** Your immediate supervisor has said something to you that you find offensive.

   Unproductive Response: "How could you be so biased? Why are you trying to hurt me?" (The Problem with This Approach: The label *biased* only serves to make the offender feel defensive. It also jumps to conclusions about the offender's intent and attitude.)

   Productive Response: "I think it is only fair to let you know that what you said made me feel very uncomfortable." (The Advantage of This Approach: It is a clear, calm statement of a feeling. It avoids blame so that the other person is better able to remain receptive to your point of view.)

5. **The Situation:** You have told someone that she has done something that hurt and offended you. She responds by saying, "Don't take things so personally; you're being too sensitive."

   Unproductive Response: "I give up. You'll never understand how I feel." (The Problem with This Response: It misses an opportunity to educate another person about respectful language and behavior.)

   Productive Response: "I realize that you and I feel differently about my reaction, but the important thing here is to sort out what happened." (The Advantage of This Response: It reframes the conversation from a focus on personal comments to the bigger issues involved.)

6. **The Situation:** You have just mentioned to one of your team that a joke she told was inappropriate and offensive. She responds with, "But no one was in the room when I said it."

   Unproductive Response: "But, you never know who might be walking by or overhear you from another room." (The Problem with This Response: It creates the impression that the only difficulty with the joke is who heard it. In fact, the joke is inappropriate regardless of who was within earshot.)

   Productive Response: "The point isn't who did or did not hear the joke. In our workplace, the goal is to treat everyone with respect and jokes like the one you told just don't support that value." (The Advantage of this Response: It redirects the conversation from the irrelevant issue of who might have heard the joke and, instead, draws attention to the overarching reason why disrespectful jokes can't be told in the workplace.)

7. **The Situation:** You want to learn more about a colleague's ethnic background or culture, but are afraid that if you ask, the person will take offense.

   Unproductive Approach: "What are you?" (The Problem with This Approach: It is abrupt and carries the connotation that the person is odd or unusual in some negative way.)

   Productive Approach: "I hope you don't mind my asking, but I'd be interested in learning more about your background." (The Advantage of This Approach: It diffuses resistance by communicating genuine interest.)

8. **The Situation:** A team member has come to you to complain of several offensive comments that her colleagues have made about her appearance. She is visibly upset and seems to be on the verge of tears.

   Unproductive Response: "Calm down. It can't be as bad as all that." (The Problem with This Response: It dismisses the woman's feelings and gives the impression that you don't trust her judgment.)

(continued)

> *Productive Response:* "I can see that this is very upsetting to you. Let's talk about it and see what we can do." (The Advantage of This Response: It communicates respect for the woman's feelings and, thereby, diffuses the emotion, allowing her to communicate more clearly.)

question, "Are you living next to any white people yet, Tony?" Politically correct? Of course not. Friends? Absolutely.

Tony's answer, by the way, to Dennis's 50-year-old question, "Why do you want to be with whites anyway?" was, "It's not that I necessarily want or don't want to be with white people. I just want to get an education so I can live anywhere I want."

CHAPTER SUMMARY

- Lowering the "volume" of both tone and words increases interest in what we have to say, maximizes credibility, and minimizes resistance to our message.
- It is tempting to make absolute or dogmatic statements in the heat of a Gateway Event. Although we all have the right to believe as we do, such statements only serve to shut down conversation and create defensiveness.
- Not every person we converse with shares our values or life history. When attempting to get your message across, use metaphors, analogies, and similes to address that individual in a way she can most readily understand.
- Listening attentively and openly is perhaps the single most important skill for dialoguing effectively about diversity.

CONCLUSION

MOMENT OF TRUTH

Each morning—well, most mornings—I roll out of bed and stagger into a room in my house that is variously called the Meditation Room, Little Man's Room (that's for my grandson, Aiden), or, in homage to my stepdaughter who once slept there, Krista's Room. I call Betsy the dog, plop myself on the floor in an awkward and painfully unnatural cross-legged sit, ring the meditation bell, and begin to do battle with my mind. That's where the dog comes in: her rhythmic breathing and inspiring ability to take life as it comes serve as constant, if at times noisy, reminders of what I am trying to accomplish.

Recently, my mind and I were engaged in a particularly bloody skirmish when I had one of those forehead-slapping insights that escape notice when one is drowning in the minutia of life. In a flash, I realized that the goal of these meditations, to take life one breath, one thought, one experience at a time, is as pertinent to reducing bias as it is to living a happier, more fulfilling existence.

As we have seen in the pages of this book, biases are distorted views of other human beings that are created by messages from the past and sustained by fear of what will happen in the future. If only we could remain in the moment—free of past messages and future fears—our vision would clear, we could see the people around us more accurately, and cases of mistaken identity would no longer weaken our ability to treat others with the respect and dignity they deserve.

My father learned this, perhaps too late to help him live a better life, but not too late to teach his children an important lesson. His revelation came during the final weeks of his life, as he lay dying in a Los Angeles hospital. Somehow the subject of bias came up—I have a vague memory it had something to do with the black man who daily swept the hall outside my father's room—and my father turned to me and admitted that he had been wrong all his life. "People are people," he said, "We have to take 'em all just one person at a time."

Reducing bias is more than just taking one person at a time, however. It is also having the patience to take one step at a time. As we saw earlier, many believe that fighting bias is a losing proposition. One reason for this pessimism is that the task seems overwhelming. In truth, our only obligation, and our only hope, is to commit to making one small gesture, after one small gesture, after one small gesture. None of us can follow Rosa Parks to that seat at the front of the bus. And few have the opportunity to defy the philosophy of an era by reaching out to a lonely stranger, like Dennis did to Tony. The small battles, the modest displays of courage, the day-to-day gestures of respect are, however, available to us all.

I witnessed one such gesture at a diversity workshop, when a young woman asked to say just one more thing before we adjourned. "It's time we begin to forgive," she said—a simple statement of healing, but a powerful one. I glimpsed another small gesture in Yoko's willingness to openly defend her male colleague against charges of sexism, despite pressure to presume him guilty until proven innocent. Perhaps, however, the gesture of bias-reducing respect that touched me most was the uncomplicated act of the father who attended a garage sale held by my family some years ago in Los Angeles. As part of an effort to rid ourselves of an obscene excess of material possessions, we had given the man's little girl one of the dozens of scarcely touched stuffed animals that my (then-grown) daughter had begged for on so many occasions. As the child, who was from Mexico, walked away, she uttered a barely audible *gracias,* to which the father responded, in an obvious effort to communicate respect for a stranger, "No, say 'thank you.'"

The practice of every technique in this book would benefit from this ability to attack bias in small, well-crafted steps, and to live life and its challenges one moment at a time. What better way to achieve the empathy discussed in the chapter "Identify Common Kinship Groups" than to stay present, in the moment, with the person with whom we are trying to connect. What more effective posture could there be for accurately assessing someone's intent during a Gateway Event than by staying in the present with that person, rather than in the past with those who have hurt us before. Finally, how better to be aware of our biased thoughts than by staying in the moment and listening quietly as they pass through our consciousness.

Like shoving biases aside, being in the moment is a habit. I know it's a habit because most of us have been habituated to the opposite behavior since childhood. For years, we have allowed, and even encouraged, our minds to jump from subject to subject, and from past to present to future. It is time we work to break that habit and focus on the now and on the individual before us. It is time we see people for who they are.

READER'S GUIDE

This Reader's Guide consists of brief summaries of each chapter followed by questions designed to encourage further dialogue and thought. The guide serves two functions. First, it allows readers to review what they have read and thus enhances the learning process. Second, it enables facilitators of diversity and bias-reduction workshops to foster in-depth discussions of the causes and cures of bias.

PART ONE: THE BASICS OF BIAS

Chapter 1: Bias Busting: It Can Be Done

Chapter Summary: Scientific evidence is mounting that biases can be controlled by using the rational parts of the brain. One group of researchers, for example, has found that if we give ourselves just a bit more time before reacting to a group, there is a good chance that our rational brain will take over and diffuse any instinctive biased reaction we might otherwise have had. Another researcher has established that the asking of specific questions forces us to see people as individuals, not as members of a group against which we have a bias. Still others have found that, although human beings are hardwired to categorize people into groups, we can quickly and easily shift individuals from one category to another.

Dialogue Questions:

1. Do you really believe that biases can be defeated?
2. Have you ever had an experience in which close contact with a member of a group allowed you to overcome your bias?
3. Have you ever had a bias-reducing experience that supports the findings of the studies found in this chapter?
4. Do you tend to put people in categories? Why do you think we do this?
5. Based on the studies discussed in this chapter, what can you think of that you or your colleagues might do in the workplace to help defeat bias?

Chapter 2: "But Everybody Does It"

Chapter Summary: No group is blameless when it comes to bias. Biases are found in all cultures, are held by both genders, and are just as apt to be harbored by a person with a disability as by someone who is fully abled. In short, despite the fact that the biases held by the more powerful "majority" populations are apt to create more damage, we all share the responsibility to work toward the goal of becoming bias free.

Dialogue Questions:

1. How do you feel about the idea that members of any group are capable of being biased? Do you resist this idea? Do you accept it?
2. Do you see any differences in impact or significance between biases held by what we call "minority" groups and those held by the dominant population?
3. Should biases held by any one group be treated differently than biases held by another?

Chapter 3: Bias Defined and Misdefined

Chapter Summary: A bias is an inflexible positive or negative belief about a particular category of people. There are many misunderstandings about what bias is. An action, for example, cannot be biased; only attitudes are biased. Furthermore, a given action or thought may or may not be proof of, or reflect, a biased attitude.

For example, being drawn to someone like oneself, mistaking one member of an unfamiliar group for another, and making a reasonable assumption about someone in light of current evidence are not necessarily evidence of bias.

Just as some actions and attitudes are mistaken as bias, others, such as biases about desirable characteristics and Guerilla Bias, are overlooked. Guerilla Biases often go undetected because, like guerilla warriors who lie concealed behind beautiful trees, these biases are hidden behind what appear to be positive actions. Based on the premise that emerging group members are in need of special treatment, this kind of bias can be manifested in actions such as failing to coach an employee who needs improvement, holding emerging group members to a low standard of performance, or making unreasonable accommodations for cultural or ethnic differences.

Dialogue Questions:

1. Do you agree with the distinction between a reasonable assumption and a bias, as described in this chapter? Can you think of examples from your life or workplace in which a reasonable assumption was mistaken for a bias or vice versa?

2. This chapter lists several behaviors and argues that they do not necessarily reflect biased attitudes. Do you agree with this argument? If not, why not?

3. Much Guerilla Bias grows out of the premise that members of emerging groups, people with disabilities, and women are in some way in need of special treatment. What consequences might this attitude have for your workplace?

4. Do you agree with the premise that holding people to a low standard of performance and behavior reflects a bias? If so, what are the consequences of this attitude in the workplace? If you do not agree, why not?

5. Do you agree that it is possible for a person to have a bias against his own kinship group? What can cause this?

6. We often fail to notice biases that say that all members of a given group have some positive characteristic. Have you ever had a bias like this? What harm do such biases do in the workplace?

PART TWO: THE VISION RENEWAL PROCESS

Chapter 4: Step One—Become Mindful of Your Biases

Chapter Summary: Most of us resist admitting, even to ourselves, that we are biased. The reason for this resistance is the misguided belief that having a bias means we are no longer good people. This chapter argues that having a bias does not necessarily mean a person is bad; it means, instead, that she is trying to feel more secure in a complex and diverse world. Becoming aware of our biases is the first step in eliminating them from our thinking. The process of bias awareness and diagnosis has several elements: watching a thought that comes to mind in response to a kinship group; examining that thought to see if we would feel the same if the person involved were from another group; measuring how much emotion is attached to that thought; recalling previous experience with the group in question; analyzing how we react when our assumption proves incorrect; examining how much we do or do not notice differences between kinship groups; and observing our behaviors.

Dialogue Questions:

1. Do you agree with the premise of this chapter that having a bias does not necessarily indicate something bad about the person's fundamental character? If you do not agree, what is your argument?

2. This chapter contends that it is possible to watch the thoughts that come into our minds. Do you agree? If not, why not? Can you give examples of other situations in which you "watched your thoughts"?

3. This chapter talks about the importance of observing your emotions when establishing the presence or absence of a bias. Do you agree that most biased attitudes are accompanied by some emotion? If so, what might some of these emotions be?

4. How might the notion of too much or too little attention to differences impact relationships in the workplace? What strategies might be employed in the workplace to balance these attitudes?

5. As a manager, what might you do to help others in the workplace become aware of their biases?

Chapter 5: Step Two—Put Your Biases through Triage

Chapter Summary: To identify which biases to attack first, we need to assess how much each one is interfering with our ability to function effectively in the workplace. Biases compromise effectiveness in many areas, including hiring and retention, productivity, building of diverse teams, and sales. They can also give rise to litigation, not only in cases of blatant discrimination, but also through subtler biases that prevent us from coaching employees properly and delivering bias-free service to customers of all backgrounds.

Dialogue Questions:

1. Contained in this chapter are several ways in which biases interfere with functioning in the workplace. Can you think of any that are not included?
2. This chapter contains a discussion of how bias can interfere with employee retention. Discuss this issue and include strategies for overcoming these difficulties.
3. Hector's career has been adversely affected by his managers' bias. Discuss Hector's situation. Do you agree that it was a bias that created his difficulties? If you disagree, why? If you agree, what other options did management have when expanding its business into the Latino neighborhood?
4. This chapter talks about how the internalization of a bias—meaning that the object of the bias comes to believe it is true—can interfere with workplace success. What strategies might you propose to minimize this problem?
5. The "stereotype threat" is one of the main ways that biases cause problems in the workplace. Propose strategies for minimizing the impact of this problem.
6. Propose some ways that managers can distinguish between appropriate adjustments for cultural differences and the kind of excessive accommodation that can compromise the effectiveness of the team.

Chapter 6: Step Three—Identify the Secondary Gains of Your Biases

Chapter Summary: Most undesirable attitudes and behaviors carry with them some sort of secondary gain. If they didn't, why would we keep indulging in them? Believing in a bias is no different; we hold on to a bias because we believe—often erroneously—that it benefits us in some way. To defeat our biases, we need to identify those secondary gains and weigh them against the damage the biases cause. Some of these alleged secondary gains are the magical ability to predict the future; protection from diminished status; protection from other kinds of loss; protection from emotional pain; and an excuse to avoid the discomfort we may feel around particular groups.

Dialogue Questions:

1. Discuss the concept of secondary gain. What behaviors or attitudes, other than bias, can you think of that are accompanied by secondary gains?
2. This chapter lists several types of secondary gains that can accompany a biased attitude. Can you think of any others that are not mentioned?
3. This chapter talks about a particular type of bias called the "bias bias." Do you believe there is such a thing? If so, why? If not, why not?
4. What argument can you make that the secondary gains listed in this chapter are not really gains after all?

Chapter 7: Step Four—Dissect Your Biases

Chapter Summary: One of the most important steps in the Vision Renewal Process is to subject our biases to a strict test of logic. This means to examine how we learned each bias so as to reveal its weak foundation and faulty beginnings. In most cases, this dissection will show that the source of the bias—be it a parent, experience, or the media—was, indeed, unreliable. We often, for example, think of experience as a reliable source of information. In fact, an experience—and the bias it creates—can be distorted by the emotions we brought to the initial event. It is also helpful to ask ourselves these questions: How much actual contact have I had with the group toward which I hold a bias? How many times have I encountered people who, in fact, do not conform to my bias?

Dialogue Questions:

1. We have talked about how parents and other "tribal leaders" are sources of bias. Often the biases our parents teach are transmitted through subtle and ambiguous messages. Do you agree that it is the subtler messages of biases that are the hardest to dislodge? If so, why? If not, why not?

2. The media is obviously responsible for a great deal of bias in our culture. What strategies might you propose in the workplace to minimize this influence?

3. This chapter talks about how our initial experiences with members of other groups can be distorted by the emotions we bring to these encounters. What other factors might distort these experiences and our memory of them? How can we prevent this distortion from taking place?

4. How do you feel about the notion that some people actually latch on to negative biases as a means of creating drama in their lives? Do you think that happens often? Does that idea surprise you?

5. How might you change the mind of someone who says his bias is true because every person he has ever met conforms to what he believes?

Chapter 8: Step Five—Identify Common Kinship Groups

Chapter Summary: One effective way to minimize both consciously and unconsciously held biases is to broaden and multiply the number of kinship groups to which we belong. This works to reduce bias because, once we share a kinship group with someone, we no longer think of that person as "them"; they instantly become "us." When this shift is accomplished, we automatically begin to evaluate members of this newly created "us" more fairly and, to make matters still better, we begin to see them as individuals.

Forming a common kinship group requires that we focus less on how we differ and more on what we share. There are several ways to do this. These include keeping what we share at the forefront of our thinking; using the Magic If technique to empathize and, therefore, identify with the experiences of others; making a personal effort to have contact with people who are the objects of our biases; creating workplace opportunities for cross-group contact; and, creating and emphasizing shared goals.

Dialogue Questions:

1. This chapter talks about multiplying and broadening our kinship groups in order to convert the objects of our bias from "them" to "us." In what ways, other than those mentioned, might this be accomplished?
2. Do you agree with the premise of the Magic If? If so, how might this doctrine be applied in the workplace to improve the functioning of diverse teams?
3. The chapter argues that it is possible for anyone to empathize with the pain suffered by emerging groups. Do you agree with this statement? If not, why not?
4. What might you, as an individual, do to make contact with people who are different from yourself? Remember that in order for that contact to be most effective at reducing bias, it should be appropriately intimate, varied, equal, and goal oriented.

Chapter 9: Step Six—Shove Your Biases Aside

Chapter Summary: Once we are aware of our biases, have questioned their logic, and have attempted to broaden our own group to include others, we are prepared for the next step: shoving our biases aside so we can see people accurately. This is a mechanical act that, if practiced regularly, becomes a habit. Once that habit is formed, two things happen. First, the sheer number of times we see people as they really are begins to put pressure on our bias to fade. Second, because we see people as they really are, we begin to relate to them more appropriately. As our behavior improves, so, in turn, do the reactions from others. Gradually those positive reactions begin to weaken our bias.

Dialogue Questions:

1. This chapter talks of how the previous steps have prepared the reader for the process of shoving biases aside. What other preparation might make the shoving aside of our biases easier?

2. The practice of shoving a thought aside seems difficult to some people. How might you help others in your workplace better understand and execute this concept?

Chapter 10: Step Seven—Fake It Till You Make It

Chapter Summary: For all our best efforts, there are times when we come across a bias that is difficult to dislodge. When this happens, there is still hope. That hope lies in the simple admonition to pretend we no longer have the bias. In other words, to self-consciously behave as if our inflexible belief does not exist. Because of the principle that attitudes follow behavior, the very act of treating people with respect can extinguish both conscious and unconscious biases. The same applies to what we say. If we speak to and about people respectfully, not only will we get a better response—which, unto itself, will reduce bias—but eventually we also will begin to believe what we are saying. Similarly, biases can be reduced by forcing our brains to focus on individual characteristics and to consider non-bias-consistent options when making personnel decisions in the workplace.

Dialogue Questions:
1. Do you agree that acting as if you don't have a bias can actually help change your attitude? If not, why not?
2. If you agree that "faking it till you make it" works, how might this be encouraged in the workplace?
3. How might the words we utter help reduce bias within ourselves? On the other hand, how might what we say increase our biases?
4. How do you feel about this idea of faking actions and words as an ethical issue? Is this lying? Is it dishonest? How might others see these behaviors in the workplace?
5. This chapter mentions that we can reduce bias by "faking out" our thoughts. Do you agree with this idea? If so, what ways, others than those presented, can be employed in the workplace to take advantage of this idea?

PART THREE: GATEWAY EVENTS™: ENTERING INTO DIVERSITY DIALOGUE

Chapter 11: The Benefits of Diversity Dialogue

Chapter Summary: Although entering into conversations about diversity-related tension and bias can be challenging and frightening, the benefits far outweigh the risks. More than anything else, such conversations serve an important educational function. Not only do they allow us to share our points of view and cultural perspectives, but they also provide an opportunity to educate others about appropriate and inappropriate behaviors. Conversation also minimizes the spread of bias by making it clear that such attitudes are unacceptable.

Dialogue Questions:

1. Several benefits of engaging in Gateway Event conversations are mentioned in this chapter. Can you think of any that ought to be added to this discussion?

2. Can you think of any disadvantages to having conversations about bias? If so, under what circumstances should such conversations be avoided?

3. What arrangements might be made in your workplace to encourage people to honestly discuss the issues of bias and diversity?

Chapter 12: Getting Diversity Fit

Chapter Summary: Becoming "diversity fit" is a way of preparing ourselves for the unexpected Gateway Events that come our way. This fitness regimen involves identifying, and thus controlling, the fears and emotions that cause us to function poorly during such conversations. Fear prevents us from thinking clearly, interferes with our ability to interpret accurately what is going on, and makes it difficult to focus on present reality, rather than on past events. The particular emotion that causes all these problems may be fear of intimacy, fear of our own biases showing, fear of the other person's anger, or simply fear of being judged.

Dialogue Questions:

1. This chapter discusses several fears and emotions that tend to come upon us in the face of Gateway Events. What other emotions can you think of that were not mentioned?
2. This chapter states that identifying the emotions that interfere with effective diversity dialogue is an important strategy for minimizing their influence. What other steps might you propose for getting our emotions under control?
3. What other strategies besides than those mentioned in this chapter, might you propose for getting "diversity fit"?

Chapter 13: Cognitive Skills for Diversity Dialogue

Chapter Summary: Dialogue about bias and diversity requires certain cognitive skills if our conversations are to be successful. These skills include resisting the urge to jump to conclusions about the intent of someone who has offended us; looking at past experiences to see how they might be coloring our own reaction; setting productive goals for the conversation; recognizing that we all share the common enemy of bias; looking for, and admitting to, the mutual contributions that all participants make to any diversity conflict; and, finally, taking every conversation one small step at a time.

Dialogue Questions:

1. The issue of "intent" is central to any discussion of bias in the workplace. What, in your view, is more important, the actor's intent or the impact of her actions? What are the reasons you feel the way you do?
2. Do you agree with the view that sometimes people feel offended not because of what just happened, but because of past experiences? If not, why not?
3. It is important to set goals before entering into diversity dialogue. What goals might you add to those listed in this chapter?
4. This chapter mentions the importance of recognizing that bias is a common enemy that we all share. Do you agree with this notion? If not, why not?

5. Discuss the section "Recognize Mutual Contributions to the Problem" in terms of other ways in which individuals might contribute to a conflict around diversity and bias. What strategies might be implemented in the workplace to identify and minimize these contributions?

Chapter 14: Verbal Skills for Diversity Dialogue

Chapter Summary: Because of the often emotional nature of Gateway Events, it is important that we learn to modulate both our tone of voice and our choice of words when having these conversations. This means not only to lower our volume, but also to avoid exaggerated labels and absolute statements, which can end a conversation before it has had a chance to begin. Also, staying alert to creative communication strategies and, as in any good conversation, listening with respect and authenticity, are key to diffusing the tension of any kind of diversity dialogue.

Dialogue Questions:

1. In addition to the suggestions in this chapter, what other ideas do you have about how we can use language more effectively when engaged in a conversation about diversity or bias?
2. This chapter emphasizes the importance of softening both tone and choice of words when engaged in a Gateway Event. Do you agree with this strategy? Are there times when this approach is not the most effective?
3. Why is listening so important in good communication? What benefits does listening provide? Why is it sometimes so difficult to listen effectively?
4. This chapter mentions the importance of using creative communication strategies in order to get our point across or keep the conversation moving in the right direction. When have you successfully employed such strategies? What were the details of the situation?
5. What programs or strategies might you develop to increase the ability of your workforce to dialogue effectively about diversity?

APPENDIX B

TRAINING ACTIVITIES

The activities in this appendix are designed to support the concepts of bias reduction found throughout the book. They are based on the assumption that the facilitator has read the book and has a general understanding of the material presented there. To help with the recall of those ideas, a reference to various book locations has been included with each activity.

The list of activities provided here is obviously not definitive nor is it intended to be. It consists of exercises that I have found to be most effective in moving the bias-reduction process forward. Use this list not only as a resource, but also as inspiration for designing additional activities that will work with your specific team members.

Applications: These activities can, of course, be used in any training session. An effort has been made here, however, to provide exercises that can readily be used in short meeting formats, such as employee orientations or weekly manager meetings.

General Facilitation Tips:
1. Start slow. Initially facilitate for moderate personal disclosure. As trust is established, deeper awareness and openness can gradually be encouraged.
2. Modify all activities and discussions to fit your corporate culture, industry language, and diversity mission.
3. Be fully inclusive. Remember that these activities are intended to reduce bias among all groups and in all directions. Biases can be held by people of all backgrounds.

4. As facilitator, get in touch with your own biases and points-of-view. Be prepared to take ownership of both in front of the group, and strive not to allow either to distort your presentation.
5. Within the limits of mutual respect, remain receptive to the views of all participants, including those that may not fit perfectly with your diversity goals.
6. Be prepared to share anecdotes about your own biases and diversity-related experiences.
7. Model appropriate behavior in front of the group. If, for example, you say something you feel might have been offensive, stop immediately to apologize and/or explain.
8. Focus as much on positive bias and Guerilla Bias as on more negative prejudices. It is the former that often go unnoticed and, therefore, unfixed.

General Format: Most of these activities are divided into two steps: introspection on the part of participants followed by a sharing with the group as a whole. Whether the participants are divided into small groups or pairs for the first part of the activity depends on the size of the group, the sensitivity of the topic, and the needs of your corporate culture.

Activity 1: "Raising the Red Flag #1—First Encounters"

Primary Purpose: To create an awareness of a past experience that might be a clue to a current bias.

Secondary Purpose: To create awareness of how experiences can create biased attitudes.

Book References: Chapter 4—Step One: "Become Mindful of Your Biases"; Chapter 7—Step Four: "Dissect Your Biases" (Question 1: "Where Did You Learn Your Bias and under What Circumstances?")

Facilitator Preparation: Look at your own history to prepare an example of what you wish the participants to provide.

Facilitation Note: As with the other Red Flag activities, this exercise is not intended to identify specific biases but merely to raise awareness of possible danger areas.

Process/Instructions:

1. Instruct each participant to share an event during which she first became aware of a group different from her own. (Examples of types of difference: ethnicity, disability, country of origin, race, religion, or sexual orientation.)
2. Ask her to talk about such details as the following: At what age did the event take place? How much time did she spend with the group in question? What were the elements of the event (for example, who was involved and what actions took place)? How did that experience impact her attitudes toward the group today?

Activity 2: "Raising the Red Flag #2—Identifying the Feeling"

Primary Purpose: To create awareness of any feelings that might constitute clues to a currently held bias.

Book References: Chapter 4—Step One: "Become Mindful of Your Biases" (Strategy III: "Measure the Emotional Intensity of Your Thoughts")

Facilitator Preparation: Beginning with the following examples, prepare a handout of questions that are appropriate to your group, your culture, and where you stand in the diversity process.

Facilitation Note: As with the other Red Flag activities, this exercise is not intended to identify specific biases, but merely to raise awareness of possible danger areas. As you ask the group for an emotion, encourage them to dig for something more specific than just generalized discomfort. (Sample emotions: fear, excitement, affection, embarrassment, or awkwardness.) Tell the group that this emotion can be negative or positive. Also, *although I would not mention this to the group,* it is possible that there will be no emotion at all. This lack of an emotional response is a positive outcome because it diminishes the likelihood that a bias is present.

Process/Instructions:

1. Post and/or hand out the questions you have prepared.
2. Instruct participants to write down any feeling they may have in response to each question. Make it clear that their answers will not be handed in and that anything they choose to share will be kept completely confidential. Also, emphasize that the feeling they come up with does not automatically mean that they have a bias. Point out, instead, that the emotion simply serves as a warning that this is an area to which they need to pay careful attention.
3. After the participants are finished, call for volunteers to share their answers.

Suggested Questions:

- When I am around a person who speaks with a heavy accent, I feel . . .
- When I meet someone who is blind, I feel . . .
- When I meet a person in a wheelchair, I feel . . .
- When I meet a person who does not speak English, I feel . . .
- When I am around people in the workplace who are much older than myself, I feel . . .
- When I am around people in the workplace who are much younger than myself, I feel . . .

Activity 3: "Raising the Red Flag #3—Family Values"

Primary Purpose: To create an awareness of deeply rooted values that might give rise to biases.

Secondary Purpose: To identify what we share.

Book References: Chapter 4—Step One: "Become Mindful of Your Biases"; Chapter 7—Step Four: "Dissect Your Biases"

Facilitator Preparation: Prepare your own example of a family story, and identify the values that the story reflects. Also, think about how those values might impact your judgments of others today.

Facilitation Note: As with the other Red Flag activities, this exercise is not intended to identify specific biases, but merely to raise awareness of possible danger areas. Also, this activity is not intended to imply any criticism of the values raised.

Process/Instructions:
1. Instruct participants to share stories that grew out of their family background. (Examples: a story about how the family arrived in this country; a tale of a colorful relative; an anecdote about a crisis or achievement that happened within the family.) To get the group started, provide a sample from your own background.
2. Instruct the group to discuss the values reflected in those stories. (Examples: hard work, punctuality, emotional openness, formality, informality, fitness, and risk taking.)
3. Have the group discuss how those values might affect their judgments of others today. (Examples: a value of physical fitness might cause a person to look down on those who are overweight; a value of risk taking might make him judgmental of people from cultures in which saving face is of great importance; a value of saving face might make her judgmental of those from cultures in which risk taking is a higher value.)

Activity 4: "Getting Unstuck"

Primary Purpose: To create awareness of the fact that once we think of a person in positive or negative terms, it is difficult to evaluate him in any other way.

Secondary Purpose: To help participants understand the heavy price we pay for our biases.

Book Reference: Chapter 5—Step Two: "Put Your Biases through Triage"

Facilitator Preparation: Think of an example in your own life that you can use to illustrate this activity.

Facilitation Note: In this version of "Getting Unstuck," participants are invited to write down the initials of someone in their personal lives whom they greatly admire and someone whom they dislike. If your participants are in people-management positions, you might have them focus instead on the member of their team who is the best performer and the person who is the worst.

Process/Instructions:

1. Ask participants to write down the initials of a person in their lives whom they very much admire. Then have them write down the initials of a person whom they dislike and disrespect.
2. After the initials of the most admired person, instruct participants to record qualities that they *dislike* about that person.
3. After the initials of the least admired person, instruct participants to record qualities that they *like* about that person.
4. Facilitate a group discussion in which you address the following questions:
   A. Did you have any difficulty coming up with negative things to say about your most admired person? (Facilitator: In most cases, they will say yes.)
   B. Did you have any difficulty coming up with positive things to say about your least admired person? (Facilitator: In most cases, they will say yes.)
   C. Why do you think you had so much trouble thinking of qualities that run against your fundamental view of each person? (Facilitator: The answer is that once we feel strongly about what someone is like, it is difficult to see her in any other way.)
   D. How does this phenomenon relate to bias? (Facilitator: The answer is that once a bias dictates a positive or negative view of an individual, we tend to think either only positive or negative things about him.)

E. What harm might this tendency to "get stuck" do to our relationships with others and the proper functioning of the workplace?

Activity 5: "Kinship Groups Galore"

Primary Purpose: To call attention to the variety of kinship groups to which each of us belongs.

Secondary Purpose: To demonstrate the number of kinship groups we, despite our differences in other ways, already share.

Book Reference: Chapter 8—Step Five: "Identify Common Kinship Groups"

Facilitator Preparation: Construct a list of groups to which the participants in your group might belong. Remember that a kinship group can be any population that shares a common interest or identity. (Examples: golfers, people who own a cat, people who are adopted, white people, immigrants, people born in another state, people who are middle children, those who share an astrological sign, people who have particular functions in your organization.) The options are limitless.

Facilitation Note: This activity has the advantage of getting participants on their feet and moving around.

Process/Instructions:

1. Instruct participants to stand in a circle. If the room is not large enough to accommodate a circle, ask them to remain seated and stand as the name of each group is called.
2. Call out names of the groups you have listed, one by one. As each person hears a group to which he belongs, he is to either step forward into the center of the circle or stand up. (Note: If you intend to give out the prize as noted below, ask each person to keep track of the number of groups to which he belongs; that is, the number of times he stepped forward or stood up.)
3. If the group in the center of the circle, on any given round, is visibly diverse, ask the participants to notice that diversity. This

drives home the point that, despite our visible differences, we all share a great deal more than we realize. That sharing is manifested in the kinship group that caused otherwise diverse people to enter the center of the circle.

4. (Optional) Award a prize to the person who is a member of the most kinship groups.
5. Explain the concept of a kinship group to the participants and how identifying shared groups can reduce bias.
6. Invite a discussion about how shared kinship groups can be identified and encouraged in the workplace.

Activity 6: "What I'd Like You to Know about Me Is . . ."

Primary Purpose: To create a sense of empathy and, therefore, a shared kinship group between people of diverse backgrounds. This sense of commonality will, in turn, help reduce bias.

Secondary Purpose: To break down biases, by educating participants about the feelings and backgrounds of their colleagues.

Book Reference: Chapter 8—Step Five: "Identify Common Kinship Groups" (Strategy II: "Practice Skills for Achieving Empathy")

Facilitator Preparation: Using your own kinship group, prepare a sample presentation in which you respond to the topics on the list below.

Facilitation Note: This activity is designed to create empathy in all directions among the kinship groups represented. It is not, for example, designed only to help men empathize with the experiences of women—but the other way around as well.

Process/Instructions:
1. Explain the purpose of this activity and the concept of kinship group.
2. Post and/or distribute the topics you have prepared. Explain that each participant will be addressing each topic as it pertains to his kinship group.

3. Instruct participants to decide which one of their own kinship groups they would like to discuss. It is suggested that they look over the list of topics first as the items there might impact their decision. Emphasize that, for purposes of this activity, it would be most valuable if they pick a group that reflects a primary dimension of diversity. (Examples: gender, age, race, national origin, ethnicity, sexual orientation, or disability.)

4. Before the first person speaks, explain to the group that they are to look for areas of commonality between what the speaker says and their own experience. Emphasize that the extremity of the shared experience or emotion does not need to be the same, merely that it is similar in some way.

5. Go around the room and have individuals talk about their chosen kinship group, according to the topics on the list. Alternatively, you can spread out the activity by selecting one person to speak each time you have a scheduled management meeting.

6. After each person speaks, invite participants to discuss ways in which they have had similar experiences or emotions. This is particularly valuable if those who raise commonalities are from primary kinship groups that are different from the speaker. (Example: a young woman listening to a middle-aged man speak about his "white male" kinship group may find common experiences, or feelings, despite the gender and age difference.)

7. Encourage participants, once they return to the workplace, to build on the commonalities that this activity has brought to light.

Suggested Questions:

- One thing I wish people knew or understood about my kinship group is . . .
- One thing that might surprise you about my kinship group is . . .
- One aspect of my kinship group I like is . . .
- One aspect of my kinship group I don't like is . . .
- If I had to change kinship groups, I would change to . . .
- What I never want to again hear about my kinship group is . . .

Activity 7: "The Question Game"

Primary Purpose: To create an awareness of commonalities with people whom we normally think of as different from ourselves. This sharing, in turn, will help reduce bias by creating a sense of common kinship group.

Book Reference: Chapter 8—Step Five: "Identify Common Kinship Groups"

Facilitator Preparation: Beginning with the questions that follow, prepare a list of items that are appropriate to your corporate culture and diversity goals.

Facilitation Note: Be prepared to call attention to the numerous commonalities that this activity brings to light.

Process/Instructions:

1. Invite a volunteer to function as the "primary responder" to the questions you supply. If time allows for more than one person to be the responder, try to achieve as much visible diversity as possible among those chosen.

2. Select five questions from the list you have prepared. As you ask each question out loud, have both the primary responder and the rest of the group write down their answers. (Note: Depending upon the time allotted and the size of the group, the number of questions asked can be increased or decreased.)

3. After all the questions are asked, have the primary responder provide his answers, one by one. After he reads each response, ask the audience if any of their answers are similar to those provided by the speaker. If so, have them share the details. Point out that we have a lot more in common than we realize. This point is particularly powerful if the two people who answered similarly are in other ways very different from each other.

4. Discuss the idea of shared kinship groups and how even answering a question the same way creates a kinship group around the values, tastes, and interests reflected in that answer.

5. Encourage participants, once they return to the workplace, to build on the commonalities that this activity has brought to light.

Suggested Questions:

- What would you like to have written on your tombstone?
- What is your favorite city, and why?
- What single non-living item would you rescue from a fire, and why? The item needs to be very specific (for example, not "photograph," but an individual photograph).
- If you could have a T-shirt printed with any message, what would that message be?
- What do you remember about your favorite holiday or tradition?
- What one piece of advice did your parents give you?
- If you could change any one thing about your life, what would it be?
- If you could go anywhere for two weeks, where would it be?
- If you could live any time in history, including now, when would that be, and why?
- If you could have lunch—just one-on-one—with any living person whom you currently do not know, who would that be?
- What one item, other than a boat, would you take to a deserted island?
- If you could change one thing about your primary culture, what would it be?
- If given a million dollars to spend freely, how would you spend it?
- What one person, living or dead, do you most admire?
- What talent would you most like to have?
- What are you most proud of about yourself or your achievements?
- If you could live anywhere, where would that be?
- Where do you fall in birth order in your family? What do you like and not like about that position?
- If you could be anyone in history, whom would that be?
- If you had to compare yourself to any animal, what animal would you pick?
- Excluding your own, whom would you most like to be your parents, and why?
- If you could use one adjective to describe yourself, what would it be?

Activity 8 (Versions A, B, C): "Did You Feel It, Too?"

Primary Purpose: To create empathy and, therefore, common kinship groups, through an awareness of shared emotions and life experiences.

Book References: Chapter 8—Step Five: "Identify Common Kinship Groups" (Strategy II: "Practice Skills for Achieving Empathy")

Facilitation Note: This activity is based on the principle of the Magic If as discussed in Chapter 8. The Magic If is a strategy for building empathy and, therefore, a shared kinship group between people who otherwise are very different from each other. Activity 8 is presented here in three versions: A, B, and C. The fundamental format of all three is the same: Participants listen to, or read, a vignette and then attempt to empathize by identifying in themselves a similar experience or emotion. As you give the instructions for all three versions, emphasize that what we are after is recognition of a shared type of emotion or experience. The emotion the responder feels does not, however, need to be as extreme as that reflected in the initial event.

Version A: "Did You Feel It, Too?"—Self-generated Events

Facilitator Preparation: Prepare an instance from your own life that can serve as an example to the group.

Facilitation Note: It is suggested that the initial sharing described here be done in pairs, triads, or small groups. This step would be followed by discussion with the group as a whole. The event/emotion can be about any aspect of living—it does not have to have anything to do with bias or diversity—and it can be positive or negative.

Process/Instructions:
1. Explain to the group the principle of the Magic If.
2. Divide the participants into pairs, triads, or small groups.
3. Instruct one person in each group to describe a positive or negative experience to which she had a strong emotional reaction. Emphasize

that the most important part of this sharing is not so much the details of the story but the feelings that the event evoked.

4. As other members of the group listen to the story, they are to look within their own history to see if they have had similar experiences or have shared similar emotions.
5. If the group is divided, reconvene for discussion: What unexpected similarities did you uncover? How did this feel? What new empathy-based kinship groups did you identify?
6. Encourage participants, once they return to the workplace, to build on the commonalities that this activity has brought to light.

Version B: "Did You Feel It, Too?"—Thumbnail Case Studies

Facilitator Preparation: Using the examples listed below as a starting point, prepare thumbnail cases that reflect your diversity goals. The incidents depicted do not have to be diversity- or bias-related events and can be either positive or negative.

Facilitation Note: This activity is particularly appropriate to use in short management meetings or employee orientation sessions.

Process/Instructions:
1. Explain to the group the principle of the Magic If.
2. Read one or more minicase studies to the participants.
3. Ask the participants to comment on ways in which they, as individuals, might have had similar emotions or experiences.
4. If the group has been broken up, call them back together and discuss the examples of empathy that this activity revealed.
5. Call attention to any similar reactions that people from diverse groups might have had to these events.

Sample Thumbnail Events:
- **Case 1:** Trieu arrived in this country as a child and immediately enrolled in public school. Because his fifth-grade teacher could not pronounce his name, she renamed him Terry. Trieu felt ambivalent about what the teacher did. On the one hand, he was proud to be an American; on the other, he felt that his ethnic identity was being ignored.

- **Case 2:** Hal worked hard in college but was unable to get a job after graduation because affirmative-action policies gave preference to women and minorities. He felt frustrated and angry.
- **Case 3:** Susan was invited to an elegant banquet and wanted to look her best. However, because of her wheelchair, she could not get up the steps to her hairdresser—there was no access for people with disabilities. Susan felt excluded, frustrated, and embarrassed.
- **Case 4:** Henry's plans for the future received a big boost when he won $150,000 in the lottery. At first, everyone at work seemed happy for him. But, after a while, he realized that most resented his good fortune.
- **Case 5:** No one can deny that Cindy is a beautiful woman. Because of that beauty, she has trouble being taken seriously in her workplace. Despite her advanced degrees and talent, many of the people with whom Cindy works feel she got where she is because of her appearance, not because of her skills.
- **Case 6:** The year was 1963, and Greg had just arrived in this country. We find him standing outside a pair of "colored" and "whites only" bathrooms in Mississippi, gazing down at the brown skin on his arm, wondering which bathroom to use.
- **Case 7:** Mark was presenting a new idea at the last departmental meeting when, after getting through only a few sentences, he was interrupted by his supervisor. She said that his idea was not well thought out and that she had a better one.

Version C: "Did You Feel It, Too?"—Full-length Case Studies

Facilitator Preparation: Beginning with the cases presented here, prepare cases that are appropriate to your group, your culture, and your diversity goals. The incidents depicted do not have to be diversity- or bias-related events and can be either positive or negative.

Process/Instructions:
1. Explain to the group the principle of the Magic If.
2. Read one or more case studies to the participants.
3. Ask the participants to comment on ways in which they, as individuals, might have experienced similar emotions or experiences.

4. If the group has been broken up, call them back together and discuss the examples of empathy that this activity revealed.

5. Call attention to any similar reactions that people from diverse groups might have had to these events.

Facilitation: Note: Following each case study, I have put a sampling of possible ways in which workshop participants might empathize with the person in the story. These are here mostly to help the facilitator understand what we are asking from the participants. Unless absolutely necessary, I suggest these sample ideas not be shared with the group as they may stifle participants' efforts to generate their own unique responses.

Suggested Case Studies:

• **Case 1—Mr. Wong (in his own words):** When I first came to America, I wanted a job as a waiter very badly. But, in order to get the job, I needed to learn English. Because I worked six and a half days out of every week, from eight in the morning to midnight, it was impossible to go to school. One of my friends suggested, "Why don't you get a dictionary?" Well, I took the advice of these young fellows and I got myself a dictionary. I think I carried that dictionary for three or four years in my back pocket just like a pack of cigarettes.

I walk on the street and I see a word and I bring out my dictionary and I find out what that word means. So when I learn one word and two and three, in time I build my own sentences; and I learn my own language that way. If you accumulate words like the way you put money in the bank two words in your notebook a day, 365 days a year, you will learn over 700 words in one year. From 700 words, that's all you need to get around; and from 700 words you can build thousands of sentences. And this is how I did it.[1]

Sample Elements/Emotions: Work ethic; ingenuity; taking a project one step at a time; determination; overcoming obstacles

Sample Empathy Event: A time you worked against all odds to achieve a milestone in your chosen athletic event.

• **Case 2—Frank (in his own words):** I'll admit it, in some ways I've had it great: I'm a white male; my parents had money; my mother was there every day after school; I went to the best universities. I really do appreciate all that, but I hate it when people act as if I've had happiness handed me on a silver platter just because I'm a relatively rich white guy. The other day, in fact, some of my colleagues at work came right out and told me how easy I've had it compared to them. Well, that might be true, but what they don't know and never will is that I've also had things to overcome. For one thing, I had an alcoholic father who, despite his financial success, vented his frustrations by regularly hitting my mother and myself. I don't like talking about it much, but my life hasn't been as easy as people think.

Sample Elements/Emotions: Feelings of being misunderstood and unappreciated; frustration

Sample Empathy Event: You are a black woman who has struggled against all odds to become a vice president at your company. However, no matter how much skill and knowledge you show, people think you are there solely because the company wants a black executive.

- **Case 3—Felipe:** When Felipe opened the gift from his in-laws—a puppet of Fidel Castro—he knew they were just trying to make a joke and show camaraderie for his Cuban heritage. However, after what the dictator had done to his family, it was no laughing matter. He had to find a way to tell them that he appreciated the gesture, but that he would be unable to display the gift and might try to find a way to sell it.

  Sample Elements/Emotions: Pride; embarrassment; the struggle not to hurt someone's feelings

  Sample Empathy Event: Some years ago, your best friend gave you a painting that very much reflects her cultural style and taste. Unfortunately, your tastes are different. She visits often so you can't just store the picture in the garage. You have a problem.

- **Case 4—Henry:** Henry, a white native-born American, is confused. His confusion is with him every day as he struggles to decipher the changing rules of the game that no longer make his role clear in the community and the workplace. From whether to compliment a colleague on her dress to the perceived threat of affirmative action, Henry, who used to be so confident, doesn't know who he is anymore.

Sample Elements/Emotions: Feelings of disorientation; feelings of inadequacy; loss of power

Sample Empathy Event: You are a woman who works for a company that recently merged with another organization. Because of the merger, the corporate culture to which you were previously accustomed has changed. As a result, you now feel completely confused about what is expected of you.

- **Case 5—Lee:** Lee is a local businessman who takes time off every Friday morning to volunteer at Children's Hospital. At a recent dinner party, he happens to mention this volunteer work to the woman next to him. Apparently, the woman's young son had once spent weeks in the hospital battling cancer. She turns to Lee and says, "I never would have made it through that ordeal without the help of the volunteers. Thank you so much for what you do."

  Sample Elements/Emotions: Pride; feelings of being appreciated; satisfaction

  Sample Empathy Event: Knowing that it is her first day, you stop by the new hire's cubicle to say hello and make her feel welcome. Two years later, you pass her in the hall and she tells you how frightened she was that day and how much that gesture meant.

- **Case 6—Steve (in his own words):** As a child, I and all the other kids at the blind school wanted nothing more than to be like other children. Through the years, we experimented with lots of ways to achieve this unlikely goal. One time, for example, a friend and I decided to pretend that we could see. We were determined to venture out alone—just the two of us—and walk down the street in such a way that no one could guess that we weren't sighted.

  To achieve this impression, it was important that we not hold on to each other. I shudder now to think how we looked. The strategy was to walk with arms at our sides (like we imagined sighted people to do) and maintain our sense of direction by occasionally brushing arms as we moved. This may have fooled the people walking past us, but it didn't do us much good when it came to navigating safely around the obstacles that sighted people take for granted. My friend, clinging to an ice-cream cone, fell straight down an open utility hole. When he pulled himself out, uninjured and unbowed, the only thing that bothered him was that he had lost his cone!

Sample Elements/Emotions: Feelings of being left out; the pressure to pretend to be something you are not

Sample Empathy Event: You once pretended to like golf in order to impress the executives of your company.

- **Case 7—Elena:** Without a trace of self-pity, Elena recounted how she was ignored when trying to make a purchase at a department store. Apparently the clerk felt that the elegantly dressed English-speaking customer standing behind Elena was more worthy of her attention than the Mexican immigrant who didn't appear to speak much English. The clerk's attitude was clear when she deliberately reached past Elena to take the other woman's purchase.

  Sample Elements/Emotions: Embarrassment; anger; feelings of being ignored; self-doubts

  Sample Empathy Event: You didn't have many friends in high school because you were ashamed to ask them over to the tiny, shabby cottage your mother rented on the edge of town.

- **Case 8—Nancy:** Nancy, a young lawyer at a prestigious male-dominated law firm, was unable to learn about important firm policies because she was excluded from the chronically all-male lunches. It is not that her colleagues were being deliberately discriminatory. They were merely indulging their natural urge to relax with people whom they perceived to be most like themselves—in this case, other men. Regardless of her colleagues' motivation, Nancy still was deprived of the valuable information she needed to succeed.

  Sample Elements/Emotions: Feelings of being left out; frustration; self-doubt; loss

  Sample Empathy Event: Upon entering college, you had high hopes for joining a particular fraternity whose members would no doubt be valuable contacts later in life. Much to your disappointment, they dismissed you early on in the rushing process. You were left with the impression that the members never really took you seriously.

- **Case 9—Robert:** Robert, who uses a wheelchair, asked his partner, Lisa, to drive him to the airport for his flight to New York City. At the last minute, Lisa decided not to just drop him at the curb like she usually does, but to park and go inside. She figured it was a good opportunity to check on some luggage she had lost on a previous flight. Once Robert got to the counter, the gate agent discovered something wrong with his reservation. Rather than talk to him directly about the problem, the agent took Lisa aside and, in hushed tones, explained the situation—as if only Lisa would understand. Whatever her motives, the agent gave the impression that she thought Robert's shriveled legs mirrored a shriveled brain as well.

  Sample Elements/Emotions: Being dismissed because of how we look; being defined by one aspect of who we are; being ignored and patronized

  Sample Empathy Event: You spent many years being what a lot of people would consider overweight. Because of that, you missed out on several job opportunities. It was as if people defined you by your body, not by the talents that you possessed.

- **Case 10—Donna (in her own words):** I've shopped in this town for 40 years and have always felt comfortable. It's not that way anymore. Many of the shops are run by the Chinese wives of the men who work at the electronics plant. I walk into these places and just don't feel welcome. I get looked up and down like I'm a thief and the salespeople ignore me. At first I decided not to go into those stores anymore, but then I said to myself, "I don't care; my money is as good as theirs."

  Sample Elements/Emotions: Anger; feelings of being out of your element; exclusion; feelings of your territory being invaded

  Sample Empathy Event: You are a recent immigrant to the United States. Although you speak fair English, you still struggle to feel at home in the culture and often find yourself excluded and looked down upon.

- **Case 11—Tom (in his own words):** I had just graduated with a master's degree in theater arts when I heard of an opening in an executive training program at a local studio. I sent my resume and followed up with a phone call. It was easy to get the human resources manager on the phone because, as he told me, I was perfect for the job. With a new baby in the other room and rent in short supply, I was very excited. "At last," I thought, "all that hard work has paid off." Then the bombshell came. "I have to ask you one thing," he said, "What is your race?" When I heard the question, my bubble burst and, judging from his tone of voice after I told him I was white, so did his. He said, "If you had been black or Hispanic, I'd hire you right this minute, but because you are white, I can't even consider your qualifications."
  Sample Elements/Emotions: Frustration; anger; feelings of inadequacy; disappointment
  Sample Empathy Event: You remember well what is was like when, at 24, you applied for your first career-track job and didn't even make it past the first round of interviews. Apparently, they wanted someone older; you never stood a chance.

- **Case 12—Rich:** Rich is a white male who has always been able to build professional contacts easily. That is until he went to work for a Chinese-owned company. Initially, Rich was optimistic about his future there, but he became discouraged when his usual charm and glibness went unappreciated. The problem? Culture and language differences were getting in his way.
  Sample Elements/Emotions: Bewilderment; feelings of inadequacy; frustration; anger
  Sample Empathy Event: You are a young female engineer who recently went to work for a male-dominated engineering firm. Although you are used to being around the opposite sex, these men are so set in their ways, you just can't figure out how to fit in.

- **Case 13—Zhao Lin Chen (in his own words):** I've only been in the United States for two years. I was a scientist in my native country. Now I have a little job—crossing guard for an elementary school.

I am very happy doing it. I came to the school in the early morning every day. I stood by the construction area outdoor, and looked at the traffic, get way for the students. Even if it is snowing or raining, I have to stay there. The people who was going and coming say hello to me. They said great while I stood on the ice in cold winter to work. Some of them gave me something for getting hot. Some time they teach me to speak English.

I met another crossing guard. It is difficult to exchange. But now we become a good friend. We talk about China, America, live, work, history, and current. He spoke slowly, and corrected my saying. I taught him to speak some Chinese. I don't have a car. He drove me to be home while it is snowing. When the weather was bad, he told me don't to ride bicycle to work. Even he pick me up to school. The weather was very cold, but my feeling was very warm. He is interesting in Chinese food. I cooked some for him to taste. I have been knew some people who was working on the construction area. Some one taught me to speak native English. Example: "Hi, brother. What's happening" I love them and my job.

Sample Elements/Emotions: Hard work; determination; pride; adaptability; self-reliance

Sample Empathy Event: Growing up in poverty taught you something about the will to succeed. Ever since then, you have actually liked challenges. For example, when working your way through school, you were proud of your job in the cafeteria even though your wealthier friends saw you clearing dishes every day.

- **Case 14—Kate (in her own words):** When I was six years old, I remember picking a flower off a neighbor's plant. This was one of those marginal sins that stays with you years after the crime. The sin was marginal because the plant wasn't actually in the neighbor's yard, but ran the length of the house separating the home from the sidewalk. Believing myself to be the complete innocent, I proudly carried my lavender treasure back home only to be told by my parents that I was guilty of theft. My father promptly scooped me up in his arms and transported me to the neighbors where I was forced to return the flower and apologize. Right then

I learned one of the guiding principles that would rule my life: the importance of telling the truth.

Sample Elements/Emotions: The value of honesty; the value of an important lesson learned; parental discipline; childhood mischief

Sample Empathy Event: You were in high school when you wrote on your hand the French words you needed for the test. No one ever found out, but, to this day, you feel a little guilty and half wish you had been caught.

- **Case 15—Joe:** Joe grew up in a lower-middle-class black community in Washington, D.C. His mother was a school teacher and his father a garage mechanic. From the very beginning, Joe showed exceptional intelligence. He attended Harvard University on an affirmative-action program and graduated at the top of his class. Joe's boss, however, could not get the idea out of her head that the only reason Joe had succeeded was affirmative action and was, therefore, utterly unable to recognize his considerable talents for what they were. Because the boss failed to give Joe opportunities for challenge and exposure, he eventually felt stifled and quit to take a vice presidency position in a parallel industry.

  Sample Elements/Emotions: Not being valued; not being trusted; being unappreciated; frustration; anger

  Sample Empathy Event: Kyle is a white male who grew up below the poverty line in rural Kentucky. Exceptionally bright despite his poor early education, Kyle had a passion for learning and toiled at menial jobs so he could attend the local college. When he finally worked his way into a good job, everyone assumed, because he was a white male, that his road had been an easy one.

ENDNOTES

Introduction

1. *Scientific American Mind,* August/September 2006.

2. *The Wall Street Journal,* November 14, 2005.

3. Bruce Jacobs, *Race Manners for the 21st Century,* (New York: Arcade Publishing, 2006), 98.

Chapter 1

1. Sharon Begley, "Racism Studies Find Rational Part of Brain Can Override Prejudice," *The Wall Street Journal* (November 19, 2004).

2. Mary E. Wheeler and Susan T. Fiske, "Controlling Racial Prejudice: Social-Cognitive Goals Affect Amygdala and Stereotype Activation," *Psychological Science* (January 2005).

3. Robert Kurzban, John Tooby, and Leda Cosmides, "Can Race Be Erased? Coalitional Computation and Social Catergorization," *Proceedings of the National Academy of Sciences* (December 18, 2001).

Chapter 3

1. Joseph G. Ponterotto and Paul B. Pedersen, *Preventing Prejudice: A Guide for Counselors and Educators,* (Newbury Park: Sage Publications, 1993), 52.

2. Nathaniel Branden, *The Six Pillars of Self-Esteem,* (New York: Bantam, 1994), 43.

Chapter 4

1. Jim Adamson, *The Denny's Story,* (New York: John Wiley & Sons, Inc., 2000), 66.

Chapter 5

1. Catalyst Inc., "The Double-Blind Dilemma for Women in Leadership: Damned If You Do, Doomed If You Don't," (2007).

2. Eileen A. Hogan, "Effects of Prior Expectations on Performance Ratings: A Longitudinal Study," *The Academy of Management Journal* (June 1987).

3. David Shipler, "Seeing Through," *The Washington Post* (May 4, 1997).

4. Ben Mezrich, *Bringing Down the House: The Inside Story of Six MIT Students Who Took Vegas for Millions,* (New York: The Free Press, 2002), 116.

Chapter 6

1. Carl Hovland and Robert Sears, "Minor Studies of Aggression: Correlation of Lynchings with Economic Indices," *The Journal of Psychology* (1940).

Chapter 7

1. Jennifer James, *Thinking in the Future Tense: A Workout for the Mind* (New York: Touchstone, 1996), 220.

2. Gordon Allport, *The Nature of Prejudice* (New York: Addison-Wesley Publishing Company, 1979), 22.

3. Paul Wachtel, *Race in the Mind of America,* (New York: Routledge, 1999), 109.

4. *Thinking in the Future Tense,* 155.

Chapter 8

1. George Harris, *Dignity and Vulnerability: Strength and Quality of Character* (Berkeley: University of California Press, 1997).

2. Mary E. Wheeler and Susan T. Fiske, "Controlling Racial Prejudice: Social-Cognitive Goals Affect Amygdala and Stereotype Activation," *Psychological Science* (January 2005).

Chapter 10

1. Daryl J. Bem, *Beliefs, Attitudes and Human Affairs,* (Belmont, California: Brooks/Cole Publishing Company, 1970), 54.

2. Jennifer James, *Thinking in the Future Tense: A Workout for the Mind,* (New York: Touchstone, 1996), 78–79.

3. *Harvard Business Review,* December 2003.

Introduction to Part Three

1. Bruce Jacobs, *Race Manners: Navigating the Minefield between Black and White Americans,* (New York: Arcade Publishing, 1999), 1.

2. *Race Manners,* 155.

Chapter 12

1. Bruce Jacobs, *Race Manners: Navigating the Minefield between Black and White Americans,* (New York: Arcade Publishing, 1999), 11.

Chapter 13

1. Douglas Stone, Bruce Patton, and Sheila Heen, *Difficult Conversations: How to Discuss What Matters Most,* (New York: Penguin Books, 1999), 46–50.

2. Solomon Moore, "Expressions of Support Surprising to Muslims," *Los Angeles Times,* September 26, 2001.

3. Roosevelt Thomas, *Building a House for Diversity,* (New York: AMACOM, 1999), 61.

Chapter 14

1. Roger Kahn, "A Tribute to Captain Courageous," *Los Angeles Times,* August 19, 1999.

2. Paul Wachtel, *Race in the Mind of America,* (New York: Routledge, 1999), 37.

3. Douglas Stone, Bruce Patton, and Sheila Heen, *Difficult Conversations: How to Discuss What Matters Most,* (New York: Penguin Books, 1999), 13.

Appendix B

1. Joan Morrison, Charlotte Fox Zabusky, et al., *American Mosaic: The Immigrant Experience in the Words of Those Who Lived It,* (Pittsburgh: University of Pittsburgh Press, 1980), 77.

INDEX